MW00752199

MANIPULATED AGENTS

MANIPULATED AGENTS

A Window to Moral Responsibility

Alfred R. Mele

OXFORD
UNIVERSITY PRESS

OXFORD
UNIVERSITY PRESS

Oxford University Press is a department of the University of Oxford. It furthers the University's objective of excellence in research, scholarship, and education by publishing worldwide. Oxford is a registered trade mark of Oxford University Press in the UK and certain other countries.

Published in the United States of America by Oxford University Press
198 Madison Avenue, New York, NY 10016, United States of America.

Library of Congress Cataloging-in-Publication Data
Names: Mele, Alfred R., 1951- author.
Title: Manipulated agents : a window to moral responsibility / Alfred R. Mele.
Description: New York, NY : Oxford University Press, [2019] |
Includes bibliographical references and index.
Identifiers: LCCN 2018032480 (print) | LCCN 2018052367 (ebook) |
ISBN 9780190927998 (online content) | ISBN 9780190927974 (updf) |
ISBN 9780190927981 (epub) | ISBN 9780190927967 (cloth : alk. paper)
Subjects: LCSH: Responsibility. | Free will and determinism. |
Act (Philosophy) | Agent (Philosophy)
Classification: LCC BJ1451 (ebook) | LCC BJ1451 .M44 2019 (print) |
DDC 128/.4–dc23
LC record available at https://lccn.loc.gov/2018032480

1 3 5 7 9 8 6 4 2

Printed by Sheridan Books, Inc., United States of America

For Joanna

CONTENTS

PREFACE

Vignettes featuring manipulated agents and designed agents have played a significant role in the literature on moral responsibility. What can we learn from vignettes of this kind about the nature of moral responsibility for actions? That is my primary question in this little book. I hope readers will find my answer and my arguments for it interesting and instructive. I hope as well that readers hoping to construct a full-blown analysis of moral responsibility will benefit from what I have to say here.

A draft of this book was among the assigned readings for a graduate seminar Oisín Deery and I taught at Florida State University in the fall semester of 2016. I am grateful to Oisín and the students for useful feedback and to Matt Flummer and Michael McKenna for written comments on that draft. I discussed a subsequent draft of this book in a seminar Michael McKenna organized at the University of Arizona in April 2017. I am grateful to the participants—especially Josh Cangelosi, Bryan Chambliss, Phoebe Chan, Michael McKenna, Nathan Oakes, Carolina Sartorio, Jason Turner, Robert Wallace, and Jonathan Weinberg—for their written and oral feedback. I am grateful as well to a pair of audiences in Budapest in March 2018—at the Central European University and the Hungarian Academy of Sciences—for discussions of themes in this book. Thanks are also owed to Gabriel DeMarco for discussion of some of the ideas in this book and to two anonymous referees for their comments. Acknowledgments of other helpful feedback appear in notes. Much of this book is based on published articles of mine. References to the article or articles on which a chapter is (partly) based appear in the final note for that chapter. Sam Sims prepared the reference section, helped design the experimental philosophy studies discussed in the Appendix, administered the studies, and did the statistical work on the results. I am grateful to him for his help. Thanks are due as well to Brad Stockdale for a final check of the reference section and other editorial assistance. This book was made possible through the support of a grant from the John Templeton Foundation. The opinions expressed here are my own and do not necessarily reflect the views of the John Templeton Foundation.

Chapter 1

Introduction

Three decades ago, Robert Kane argued that "no existing compatibilist account of freedom . . . defines freedom" in such a way as "to ensure against the success of any potential covert non-constraining (CNC) control of the agent's will by another agent" (1985, p. 37). In cases of CNC control, as Kane conceives of such control, the agent is not "constrained in the sense of being made to do things he does not want or desire to do." Instead, "the CNC controller" covertly arranges "circumstances beforehand so that the agent wants and desires, and hence chooses and tries, only what the controller intends." Kane's claim is that the compatibilist accounts of free will or free action in existence at the time lack the resources for distinguishing cases in which an agent is rendered unfree (regarding various actions) by another agent's CNC control over him from cases in which an agent acts freely or of his own free will. His libertarian strategy for blocking CNC control appeals to indeterminism. If it is causally undetermined what a particular agent will choose, he asserts, "no potential controller could manipulate the situation in advance so that the choice necessarily comes out as the controller plans or intends" (1985, p. 36). Thus, Kane contends, its being the case that an agent is not causally determined to choose what he chooses at *t* "thwarts[s] *any* potential CNC controller" intent upon controlling what the agent chooses at *t*.

(Readers unfamiliar with the technical terminology in this paragraph will find Section 1 useful.)

Kane's particular libertarian strategy for dealing with cases of CNC control—a form of manipulation—is unsuccessful, as I explain in Chapter 6 (also see Mele 1995, pp. 187–88 and 2006, pp. 52–53). But, to my mind, what is far more interesting is that there is a promising compatibilist strategy for dealing with such cases, both regarding free will and regarding moral responsibility, and the strategy can be used to good effect by libertarians as well. I developed such a strategy in Mele 1995, and I develop it further in this book.

Thought experiments about manipulation and "manipulation arguments" have received a lot of attention in the past thirty years. The relatively recent literature on these matters tends to focus on moral responsibility—especially for actions—but free will is still in the picture. This book's guiding question is about moral responsibility: What can we learn about the nature of moral responsibility for actions from reflection on thought experiments featuring manipulation (and related thought experiments)?

1. SOME TERMINOLOGY

Brief remarks on terminology are in order. I start with *compatibilism*. In terms of possible worlds, compatibilism about free will and determinism, as I understand it (following standard practice), is the thesis that there are possible worlds in which determinism is true and free will exists. *Incompatibilism* is the denial of compatibilism. If free will is possible but absent in all possible worlds in which determinism is true, incompatibilism (about free will) is true. Incompatibilism (about free will) also is true if free will is impossible. (Most incompatibilists take free will to be possible.) In both cases, there is no possible world in which determinism is true and free will exists. Similarly, in terms of possible worlds, compatibilism about moral responsibility and determinism is the thesis that there are possible worlds in which determinism is true and moral responsibility exists; and incompatibilism is the denial of this thesis.[1] (For the record, I am officially agnostic about compatibilism, both about free will and about moral responsibility; see Mele 1995, 2006, 2017.) *Libertarianism* is the conjunction of two claims—the claim that incompatibilism about free will is true and the claim that free will exists. If moral responsibility is absent in all possible worlds in which free will is absent, as is often assumed (see Mele 2015), then libertarianism has implications for moral responsibility.

Peter van Inwagen describes *determinism* as "the thesis that there is at any instant exactly one physically possible future" (1983, p. 3). The thesis he has in mind, expressed more fully, is that at any instant exactly one future is compatible with the state of the universe at that instant and the laws of nature. There are more detailed characterizations of determinism in the literature; but this one is fine for my purposes. (An exception may be made for instants at or very near the time of the Big Bang.)

While I am at it, I should say something about how I use the expressions "free will" and "moral responsibility." I conceive of free will as the ability to act freely and treat free action as the more basic notion. But what is it to act freely? As I observe in Mele 2006, there are readings of "*A*-ed freely" on which the following sentence is true: "While Bob was away on vacation, mice ran freely about his house" (p. 17). Such readings do not concern me. My interest is in what I call *moral-responsibility-level free action*—"roughly, free action of such a kind that if all the freedom-independent conditions for moral responsibility for a particular action were satisfied without that sufficing for the agent's being morally responsible for it, the addition of the action's being free to this set of conditions would entail that he is morally responsible for it" (p. 17).[2] As I understand moral responsibility, an agent's being morally responsible for performing good or bad intentional actions of the sort featured in the stories presented in this book entails that he deserves some moral credit or moral blame for those actions.[3] I take no position on exactly how moral credit and moral blame are to be understood. But I follow Derk Pereboom when I report that the desert I have in mind does not derive from consequentialist or contractualist considerations (2014, p. 2).

I take seriously both words in the expression "morally responsible." As I understand moral responsibility, it is a moral matter. So, in my view, agents are not morally responsible for actions that fall outside the sphere of morality—or, more precisely, actions that morality is not in the business of prohibiting, requiring, or encouraging. (I owe this way of putting things to Josh Gert.)

A positive effect of recent metaphilosophical attention to intuitions and their place in philosophy is increased caution in first-order philosophy about how one uses the term "intuition," a term used in a variety of different ways by philosophers (see Cappelen 2012). In this book, I use the term "intuition" specifically in connection with reactions to cases. In this context, what I have in mind are beliefs and inclinations to believe that are relatively pre-theoretical. These beliefs and inclinations are not arrived at by consulting one's favorite relevant philosophical position and applying it to the case at hand, and they sometimes prove useful when one attempts to test philosophical analyses or theories by testing their implications about cases. I definitely do not regard intuitions as the final word. We may question, test, and reject our own intuitions about cases. I also have no wish to tell others how they should use the word "intuition."

2. INTERNALISM AND EXTERNALISM: SETTING THINGS UP

Here is a truism. All actual human agents who perform intentional actions are influenced by things they have done and things that have happened to them.[4] If an actual agent is a superb deliberator or remarkably courageous, we might like to know how he came to be that way, if only because that knowledge about his past might suggest measures we might take to make ourselves better deliberators or more courageous. The central question to be explored in this book about the bearing of an agent's history on whether he is morally responsible for an action, *A*, that he performed (and here I count deciding to do something and deliberating about what to do as actions) is a question about whether things the agent did and things that happened to him before "the relevant time" have a "certain kind" of bearing on whether he is morally responsible for *A*.[5] When does the relevant time begin? For my purposes here, the following answer will do: shortly before his *A*-ing begins. (Bear in mind that most actions are not momentary events; hence the reference to his *A*-ing's *beginning*.) And what kind of bearing is at issue? I get to that shortly.

Imagine that you have decided to construct an analysis of "*S* is morally responsible for *A*-ing," where *S* is a placeholder for any possible agent and *A* is a placeholder for any possible action. In your thinking, you might start with what you regard as paradigmatic cases of actions for which ordinary human beings are morally responsible. Eventually, you would come to a question about agents' histories that lies at the heart of this book.

An efficient way to introduce this question is by way of a couple of quotations from work by Harry Frankfurt:

> To the extent that a person identifies himself with the springs of his actions, he takes responsibility for those actions and

> acquires moral responsibility for them; moreover, the questions of how the actions and his identifications with their springs are caused are irrelevant to the questions of whether he performs the actions freely or is morally responsible for performing them. (Frankfurt 1988, p. 54)

> If someone does something because he wants to do it, and if he has no reservations about that desire but is wholeheartedly behind it, then—so far as his moral responsibility for doing it is concerned—it really does not matter how he got that way. One further requirement must be added: . . . the person's desires and attitudes have to be relatively well integrated into his general psychic condition. Otherwise they are not genuinely his . . . . As long as their interrelations imply that they are unequivocally attributable to him . . . it makes no difference—so far as evaluating his moral responsibility is concerned—how he came to have them. (Frankfurt 2002, p. 27)

Frankfurt is claiming here that as long as an agent is in a certain internal condition when he *A*-s, he is morally responsible for *A*-ing, no matter how he came to be in that internal condition. An agent's *internal condition* at a time may be understood as something specified by the collection of all psychological truths about the agent at the time that are silent on how he came to be as he is at that time.[6]

Frankfurt's main thesis in these passages (for my purposes) has the following form: If an agent is in internal condition *C* when he *A*-s and he *A*-s because of a part *P* of *C*, then he is morally responsible for *A* no matter how he came to be in *C*. Theses of this form—*form F*—express versions of what I dub *conditional internalism*. As I understand conditional internalism, theses with the form of simplified variants of *F* that include no reference to any part of *C* or have no "because" clause at all also express versions of conditional internalism. For example, a thesis with the following form is a conditional internalist thesis: If an agent is in internal condition *C* when he *A*-s, then he is morally responsible for *A* no matter how he came to be in *C*.

Many different versions of conditional internalism can be put forward as rivals to Frankfurt's own version of the view. The main substantive differences between them will lie in how *C* is filled in. Frankfurt contends that an agent's being in a particular internal condition when he *A*-s is sufficient for his being morally responsible for *A*-ing. A philosopher who rejects Frankfurt's own proposed sufficient condition for moral responsibility may hold that being in some other internal condition when one *A*-s is sufficient for being morally responsible for *A*-ing and that, in Frankfurt's words, "as long as" an agent is in that condition when he *A*-s, "it makes no difference—so far as evaluating his moral responsibility is concerned—how he came" to be in it (2002, p. 27). This philosopher would reject Frankfurt's proposal of a sufficient condition for moral responsibility for an action but accept conditional internalism, as Frankfurt does. My concern in this book extends well beyond Frankfurt's own view to internalism in general about moral responsibility—especially conditional internalism in general.

A bolder brand of internalism is *unconditional internalism*. This is the thesis that an agent's internal condition at the relevant time and the involvement of that condition in his *A*-ing are relevant to whether he is morally responsible for *A*, and no fact about how he came to be in that condition is relevant. Notice that whereas conditional internalists offer a sufficient condition for being morally responsible for an action, there is no mention of such a condition in my statement of unconditional internalism. Indeed, a proponent of unconditional internalism might not be committed to any particular alleged sufficient condition for an agent's being morally responsible for an action.[7]

Unconditional internalism is an unpromising view, as a little reflection on the following pair of cases shows. Van, a normal man, gets drunk at a party and then tries to drive home. He is so drunk that he does not realize he is impaired. No one tricked Van into drinking alcohol, no one forced him to drink, he is knowledgeable about the effects of alcohol, and so on. Owing to his drunkenness, he accidentally drives into and kills a pedestrian he does not see. Assume that moral responsibility is common in Van's world. With that assumption in place, a plausible judgment about Van is that, other things being equal, he is morally responsible for killing the pedestrian.[8]

Ike is just as drunk as Van when Ike tries to drive home, so drunk that he does not realize he is impaired. Owing to his drunkenness, Ike accidentally drives into and kills a pedestrian he does not see. However, Ike was force-fed alcohol and placed in the driver's seat of his car. It is very plausible that he is *not* morally responsible for killing the pedestrian.

If these asymmetrical judgments about Van and Ike are justified, what justifies them? The difference between how these agents came to be as they were when they were driving and when they killed the unfortunate pedestrians plainly would play a major role in the justification. Obviously, this is a difference in their *histories*. If the plausible judgments about Van and Ike are true, unconditional internalism is false.[9]

Just as unconditional internalism can be tested by reflection on pairs of cases, so can substantive versions of conditional internalism. Return to the passages quoted from Frankfurt's work a few paragraphs ago. The claims he makes there can be tested by comparing certain pairs of agents who satisfy the sufficient conditions he offers for being morally responsible for *A*-ing: One member of the pair comes in some normal way to be, at the relevant time, in the internal condition that Frankfurt identifies here, and the other comes to be that way at that time as a consequence of very recent heavy-duty manipulation of a sort to be discussed in subsequent chapters. My present task is to clarify the question at issue about agents' histories. The testing of conditional internalist views begins in Chapter 2.

Conditional internalism (unlike unconditional internalism) is compatible with what I call *conditional externalism*. This is the thesis that even if some conditional internalist thesis is true, agents sometimes are morally responsible for *A* partly because of how they came to be in the internal condition that issues in their *A*-ing; and, more specifically, in these cases, there is another possible way of having come to be in that internal condition such that if they had come to be in that condition in that way, then, holding everything else fixed (except what is entailed by the difference, of course), including the fact that they *A*-ed, they would not have been morally responsible for *A*. The stories about Van and Ike, as I see things, illustrate the truth of at least a conditional externalism. In subsequent chapters, I explore the question of how far-reaching a plausible conditional externalism may be.

Two points should be made about the expression "how they came to be in the internal condition that issues in their *A*-ing." The first is straightforward. In some cases, what may be most important about how agents came to be in this condition is that the way they did so *lacks* certain features. The second point concerns "instant agents," imaginary beings who come into existence with the wherewithal to act intentionally right then.[10] If such beings are conceptually possible, I will say that there is a way in which they come to be in the internal condition they are in at the first moment of their existence—namely, the instant or all-at-once way. Obviously, this is not to say that they have any agential history at this time; that requires having acted, and they have not acted yet. If some instant agents can be morally responsible for their earliest actions (a topic of discussion later), what may be important about the way in which they come to be in their internal condition at the time is that this way lacks certain features.

A theorist with the aim of developing a substantive conditional internalist proposal should either try to fill in *C* and *W* in the following statement or try to fill in *C* and explain why, with *C* in place, *W* is otiose:

> *CI*. There is some internal condition *C* such that if an agent who purposefully *A*-s is in *C* at the relevant time and *C* (or a part of *C*) accounts for *A* in internal way *W*, the agent is morally responsible for *A* no matter how he came to be in *C*.[11]

As I have mentioned, an agent's *internal condition* at a time may be understood as something specified by the collection of all psychological truths about the agent at the time that are silent on how he came to be as he is at that time. And, by definition, an *internal* accounting for *A* makes no reference to things that happened before "the relevant time."

I define *unconditional externalism* as the thesis that *CI* is false. It is among the views commented on in this book.

Philosophers sometimes distinguish between direct and indirect moral responsibility. If indirect moral responsibility for an action is possible (as I believe), my story about Van provides an example. We can say—correctly, in my opinion—that Van's moral responsibility for his accidental killing of a pedestrian is wholly inherited from his moral responsibility for other relevant actions of his. What might some of these relevant actions be? Ike's story suggests an answer. Given the details of this story, Ike is not morally responsible for killing the pedestrian. And that is partly because Ike is not morally responsible for the alcohol consumption that causally contributed to the killing. However, Van (by hypothesis) is morally responsible for his alcohol consumption in my story about him.

I will say that an agent is *directly* morally responsible for *A*-ing when and only when he is morally responsible for *A*-ing and that moral responsibility is not wholly inherited from his moral responsibility for other things. Being directly morally responsible for *A*-ing, so construed, is a matter of having at least *some* direct (that is, uninherited) moral responsibility for *A*-ing. It may be that an agent's moral responsibility for *A*-ing sometimes includes a combination of direct and inherited moral responsibility. A philosopher who distinguishes direct and indirect moral responsibility along these lines will, of course, notice that the most fundamental business of an analysis of moral responsibility for actions is to capture direct moral responsibility for actions. After that is done, the philosopher can get to work on the inheritance relation.

3. PREVIEW

I close this chapter with a brief preview of what is to come. Chapter 2 offers a critique of Frankfurt's conditional internalist view and provides some motivation for a certain kind of externalist view of moral responsibility for actions. Chapter 3 reinforces that externalist view by rebutting various critiques of it. Chapter 4 critically examines arguments for the thesis that compatibilism commits its proponents to rejecting the view of moral responsibility for actions defended in this book. Chapter 5 continues the discussion of a compatibilist view of moral responsibility for actions, paying special attention to the question of how compatibilists should respond to stories of different kinds—stories featuring manipulation and stories featuring imaginary agents who are built from scratch. Chapter 6 presents an argument for the thesis that both compatibilists and incompatibilists about moral responsibility for actions should accept the view of it advanced in this book, and it answers a variety of questions about my externalist view and my procedure in this book. The Appendix reports on some simple studies I conducted of nonspecialists' responses to some cases of manipulation.[12]

Chapter 2

Internalism and Externalism

In Chapter 1, I placed the following five options on the table.

1. Unconditional internalism: An agent's internal condition at the relevant time and the involvement of that condition in his *A*-ing are relevant to whether he is morally responsible for *A*, and no fact about how he came to be in that condition is relevant.
2. Conditional internalism: There is some internal condition *C* such that if an agent who purposefully *A*-s is in *C* at the relevant time and *C* (or a part of *C*) accounts for *A* in internal way *W*, the agent is morally responsible for *A* no matter how he came to be in *C*.
3. Frankfurt's conditional internalism.
4. Conditional externalism: Even if some conditional internalist thesis is true, agents sometimes are morally responsible for *A* partly because of how they came to be in the internal condition that issues in their *A*-ing; and, more specifically, in these cases, there is another possible way of having come to be in that internal condition such that if they had come to be in that condition in that way, then, holding everything else fixed (except what is entailed by the difference, of course), including

the fact that they *A*-ed, they would not have been morally responsible for *A*.

5. Unconditional externalism: Conditional internalism is false. (No brand of conditional internalism is true.)

Modifying "morally" with "directly" in 1, 2, and 4 results in variants of these theses that are specifically about direct moral responsibility for actions.

I have already observed that if I am right about Van and Ike, the drunk drivers in Chapter 1, then unconditional internalism is false. Unconditional internalism is at one extreme. At the other is unconditional externalism. I comment on the latter view in Section 1. In Sections 2 and 3, I present some counterexamples to Frankfurt's conditional internalism. In Section 4, I forge ahead in preparing the way for a version of conditional externalism.

1. UNCONDITIONAL EXTERNALISM AND MABEL

The term "values" appears in stories to be spun in this chapter. Some background on my use of this term is in order. In Mele 1995, I complain that philosophers often leave it to their readers to guess what they mean by "values," and I offer glosses on the verb and the noun. As I understand valuing there, "*S* at least *thinly values X* at a time if and only if at that time *S* both has a positive motivational attitude toward *X* and believes *X* to be good" (p. 116).[1] When values are understood as psychological states, I take them to have both of these dimensions by definition. This account of thinly valuing and the corresponding thin account of values are not meant to be contributions to the theories of valuing and values; their purpose is simply to make my meaning clear. Recall Robert Kane's claim, mentioned in

Chapter 1, that in the cases of manipulation that especially interest him, the agent is caused to want to do what the manipulator wishes him to do (1985, p. 37). In the main cases of manipulation that I develop, implanted values (or their physical realizers or facts about what the agent values) make important causal contributions to what the agent does.[2] The positive motivational attitudes to which the quotation on valuing from Mele 1995 refers are desires (in a broad sense familiar in the philosophy of action; see Mele 2003a, chap. 1).

I turn now to unconditional externalism. Meet Mabel. One of the features of her internal condition is that, no matter what change in her mental condition is produced by manipulation, as long as it does not incapacitate her, she can immediately undo it. So, for example, she can undo the effects of value manipulation at any moment: In a moment, she can erase any values produced by manipulation and produce in herself a system of values that matches, in its internal features, any system of values erased by manipulation. Indeed, her internal condition always includes the marvelous ability to produce in herself any conceivable system of values from moment to moment. Mabel also is able to act on any values that she has at a time, provided that so doing is logically possible. Her marvelous abilities enable her immediately to bring it about that she has abilities associated with values that had been erased. As Mabel knows, these marvelous abilities suffice for her being able during any time, *t*, to act on any conceivable values, provided that her acting on them during *t* is logically possible.

A presumption in my story about Mabel should be made explicit. The values ordinary adult human agents have over a span of time together with the circumstances in which they find themselves over that span constrain what it is open to them to desire then.[3] For example, in the ordinary circumstances in which my friend Bob found himself yesterday, it was open to him, given his values, to desire to take a break from work and cross the street to buy some coffee, but it was not open to him to desire to disrobe and walk naked across the street to buy coffee. If he had gone insane, he might have been capable of desiring to do that. And if aliens had persuaded him that the world would be saved only if he bought coffee in the nude, his values would have supported a desire to do that. But Bob was not capable—in the circumstances and given his values—of desiring to buy coffee in the nude. I take being able at a time to perform an intentional action, *A*, at that time, in one respectable sense of "able," to depend on a variety of things, including being capable—in the circumstances that obtain at the time and given one's values—of desiring at that time to *A* then (see Mele 1995, p. 150, on this and possible exceptions for certain kinds of action). In my view, then, the values a normal adult human agent has are relevant to what he is able at a time (in the sense at issue) to do intentionally at that time insofar as, given his circumstances, they permit him to desire at that time to do various things then or render him incapable (in the sense explained) of so desiring. (On a closely related matter, see Chapter 3, Section 3.) Many desires are *extrinsic* desires: The paradigm case is desiring something as a means to an end. To desire something *intrinsically* is to desire it for its own sake or as an end. Some such desires are desires to do things, as Bob might desire to show his appreciation to Cathy for its own sake and not for a further purpose. Desires of both kinds—extrinsic and intrinsic—are relevant in the present context.

Mabel obviously is not an actual human being. There are stories about real people who suddenly and radically transform their values. But it is a good bet that, in any credible story of this kind, there is a partial basis in the person's pre-transformation character or values for the post-transformation system of values (see Mele 2006, pp. 179–84).[4] In any case, if Mabel is a possible being, marvelous abilities like hers may be built into *C* in my generic formulation of conditional internalism in an attempt to produce a true substantive version of conditional internalism. (I do not claim that Mabel is a possible being.)

A true version of conditional internalism that includes these abilities in an agent's internal condition may not be particularly illuminating, but it would falsify unconditional externalism. I add that none of the agents in the other stories to be told in this chapter have Mabel's special abilities.

2. A PROBLEM FOR FRANKFURT

In the present section, I offer a counterexample to Frankfurt's conditional internalist proposal. The counterexample needs some stage-setting, beginning with additional commentary on abilities.[5]

An important ingredient of traditional compatibilist views is that some agents in deterministic worlds who do not *A* at *t* were able to *A* at *t* and others were not. (The claim that they "could [not] have *A*-ed at *t*" may be treated as another way of saying that they were [not] able to *A* at *t*.) Typical incompatibilists insist that an agent who did not *A* at *t* was able to *A* at *t* only if in some possible world with the same laws of nature and the same past up to *t*, he *A*-s at *t*, and traditional compatibilists deny this. One way to see the disagreement, when concerns about moral responsibility have a significant influence on the debate, is as a disagreement about the range of possible worlds to which it is permissible to appeal in a certain connection in an attempt to support a judgment that an agent who *A*-ed is—or is not—morally responsible for *A*.

What connection is that? Consider what Frankfurt calls "the principle of alternate possibilities": (*PAP*) "A person is morally responsible for what he has done only if he could have done otherwise" (1969, p. 829). Notice that *PAP* includes no temporal indices. Suppose that "could have done otherwise" in *PAP* were given a synchronic reading—that is, that *PAP* were read as follows: (*PAPs*) A person is morally responsible for what he did at *t* only if, at *t*, he could have done otherwise then.[6] Then Van's case falsifies the principle, if I am right about Van. Well before he struck the pedestrian, there was a time at which it was too late for Van to do otherwise than strike and kill him. (Indeed, some milliseconds before a sober driver accidentally strikes a pedestrian, it is too late for him to do otherwise.) One way to protect *PAP* against Van's case is to formulate it as follows: (*PAPh*) A person is morally responsible for what he did at *t* only if he was able, either before *t* or at *t*, to do otherwise at *t*. Van does not falsify this principle (at least on some reasonable readings of "able") if, for example, the following two statements are true: He was able, at some relevant earlier time, to stop drinking before he got drunk; and if he had done that, he would not have run the pedestrian down at *t*.

Now I can answer the question with which I opened the preceding paragraph. Suppose that traditional compatibilists and incompatibilists agree that *PAPh* (or some similar principle) is true. Claims that agents in a world *W* who did not *A* were able to *A* are properly tested in relevant possible worlds. Incompatibilists insist that, at least for the sorts of ability to do otherwise that are crucial to moral responsibility, the only relevant possible worlds are worlds with the same past and laws of nature as *W*. (Obviously, if *W* is a deterministic world, then in all worlds with the same past and laws as *W* the agent does exactly what he does in *W*.) Traditional compatibilists disagree. They contend that a broader range of worlds is admissible for tests of the pertinent kinds of ability. What matters for warranted attributions of these kinds of ability, they may say, is whether the agent is suitably responsive to reasons at some relevant time.

I have mentioned some traditional compatibilist ideas. Semicompatibilists are untraditional compatibilists. Consider a theorist who goes beyond the official *semicompatibilist* claim that determinism is compatible with moral responsibility *even if* determinism is incompatible with the ability to do otherwise (Fischer 1994, p. 180) to the stronger claim that determinism is compatible with moral responsibility *even though* determinism is incompatible with the ability to do otherwise (Fischer 2000, p. 328). This semicompatibilist may agree with some traditional compatibilists about the importance of reasons-responsiveness for moral responsibility while disagreeing about the connection between such responsiveness and agents' *abilities*. In this book, when compatibilism is at issue, I assume that some account of "could have done otherwise" according to which an agent in a deterministic world sometimes could have done otherwise than he did is, in principle, defensible; but some semicompatibilist *analogues* of "could have done otherwise" may be fine for my purposes.[7]

It is time to consider a pair of stories (based on stories in Mele 2006, pp. 171–72; also see Mele 1995, chap. 9). The stories do not specify whether the world in which they are set is deterministic or indeterministic.

Thoroughly Bad Chuck. Chuck enjoys killing people, and he "is wholeheartedly behind" his murderous desires, which are "well integrated into his general psychic condition" (Frankfurt 2002, p. 27). When he kills, he does so "because he wants to do it" (Frankfurt 2002, p. 27), and "he identifies himself with the springs of his action" (Frankfurt 1988, p. 54). When he was much younger, Chuck enjoyed torturing animals, but he was not wholeheartedly behind this. These activities sometimes caused him to feel guilty, he experienced bouts of squeamishness, and he occasionally considered abandoning animal torture. However, Chuck valued being the sort of person who does as he pleases and who unambivalently rejects conventional morality as a system designed for and by weaklings. He freely set out to ensure that he would be wholeheartedly behind his torturing of animals and related activities, including his merciless bullying of vulnerable people, and he was morally responsible for so doing. One strand of his strategy was to perform cruel actions with increased frequency in order to harden himself against feelings of guilt and squeamishness and eventually to extinguish the source of those feelings. Chuck strove to ensure that his psyche left no room for mercy. His strategy worked. Today, he stalked and killed a homeless man, Don. He waited until he was confident that the killing would go undetected and then slit Don's throat. Showing mercy was not an option for Chuck, and he understood that, from the perspective of conventional morality, what he did was morally wrong.

One Bad Day. When Sally crawled into bed last night, she was one of the kindest, gentlest people on Earth. She was not always that way, however. When she was a teenager, Sally came to view herself, with some justification, as self-centered, petty, and somewhat cruel. She worked hard to improve her character, and she succeeded. When she dozed off, Sally's character was such that intentionally doing anyone serious bodily harm definitely was not an option for her: Her character—or collection of values—left no place for a desire to do such a thing to take root. Moreover, she was morally responsible, at least to a significant extent, for having the character she had. But Sally awakes with a desire to stalk and kill a neighbor, George. Although she had always found George unpleasant, she is very surprised by this desire. What happened is that, while Sally slept, a team of psychologists that had discovered the system of values that make Chuck tick implanted those values in Sally after erasing her competing values. They did this while leaving her memory intact, which helps account for her surprise. Sally reflects on her new desire. Among other things, she judges, rightly, that it is utterly in line with her system of values. She also judges that she finally sees the light about morality—that it is a system designed for and by weaklings. Upon reflection, Sally "has no reservations about" her desire to kill George and "is wholeheartedly behind it" (Frankfurt 2002, p. 27). Furthermore, the desire is "well integrated into [her] general psychic condition" (Frankfurt 2002, p. 27). Seeing nothing that she regards as a good reason to refrain from stalking and killing George, provided that she can get away with it, Sally devises a plan for killing him; and she executes it—and him—that afternoon, once she is confident that the killing would go undetected. Her current view of things is utterly predictable, given the content of the values that ultimately ground her reflection, and her new system of values left no room for mercy. Sally "identifies [herself] with the springs of [her] action" (Frankfurt 1988, p. 54), and she kills George "because [she] wants to do it" (Frankfurt 2002, p. 27). Like Chuck, Sally understands that, from the perspective of conventional morality, such a killing is morally wrong. If Sally was able to do otherwise in the circumstances than attempt to kill George only if she was able to show mercy, then, because her new system of values left no room for mercy, she was not able to do otherwise than attempt to kill George. When Sally falls asleep at the end of her horrible day, the manipulators undo everything they had done to her. When she awakes the next day, she is just as sweet as ever and she has no memory of the murder.

Chuck and Sally are partial *value twins* in a certain sense. The values that issue—in the same way—in their killings have the same content, and they are just as powerful. Being partial value twins in this sense obviously is compatible with lots of psychological differences. For example, occurrent memories are psychological states, and Chuck and Sally have very different occurrent memories. Also, their sharing the values just mentioned is compatible with their not sharing some other values—for example, values concerning food and soft drinks. Hence the adjective "partial."

Both Chuck and Sally satisfy Frankfurt's conditions for being morally responsible for the deeds at issue.[8] That they differ markedly in "how [they] came to have" their relevant "desires and attitudes . . . makes no difference," according to Frankfurt (2002, p. 27). However, that is difficult to accept. While (in the absence of further details that would get him off the hook) I see Chuck as morally responsible for his killings, I cannot help but see Sally as too much a victim of external forces to be morally responsible for killing George. Frankfurt may reply that "We are inevitably fashioned and sustained, after all, by circumstances over which we have no control" (2002, p. 28). But this assertion does not entail that we "have no control" at all regarding any of our "circumstances." (Frankfurt says "by," not "by and only by.") And whereas Sally exercised no control in the process that gave rise to her Chuckian system of values and identifications, Chuck apparently exercised significant control in fashioning his system of values and identifications. Frankfurt is committed to holding that that difference between Chuck and Sally is "irrelevant to the questions of whether [they perform the killings] freely or [are] morally responsible for performing them" (1988, p. 54); and he may contend that even if many people do have some control over some of their "circumstances," Chuck is simply morally responsible for an extra item that Sally is not—having become an evil person. The contention is that both are morally responsible for the killings and kill freely, and that Chuck, but not Sally, is morally responsible for having become a ruthless killer. In my opinion, this contention is unsustainable, and if compatibilists were to have nothing more attractive to offer than Frankfurt's internalist view of moral responsibility and freedom, compatibilism would be in dire straits. I return to this issue later in this chapter and in Chapter 4.

Before I move on, I comment briefly on a strategy for attempting to show that the outlook for Frankfurt's view is not as grim as I have made out. In *One Bad Day*, Sally does not remember killing George. Suppose she did remember this. It may be claimed that, in that case, her feeling guilty about killing him would be understandable, that this feeling may be associated with her regarding herself as morally responsible for the killing, and that we are in no position to dispute Sally's position on this. A theorist might try to find a way to apply an alleged lesson from this line of thought to *One Bad Day* in an effort to undermine my verdict about that story.[9]

If I had a chance to talk to Sally in this *memory* version of the story, I would try to impress upon her the importance of distinguishing between feeling guilty about something one did and feeling terrible about something one did. Consider the following case. Ted is walking through a large, crowded living room at a party on his way to the front door. Adults are standing and talking, children are milling around, and a several babies are crawling on the carpet. Ted is carefully navigating the room when a drunk acquaintance trips him, thinking that it would be fun to see Ted fall, given how carefully he is walking. Ted does his best to avoid crashing into anyone—especially the babies—but he falls on a baby and breaks her leg.

Later, Ted tells me that he feels guilty about breaking the baby's leg. I gently suggest to him that he may be confusing feeling terrible about breaking the baby's leg, which would be entirely understandable, with feeling guilty about it. (How would you feel, dear reader, if you were in Ted's shoes? Would you feel terrible?) In any case, I tell Ted that he should not feel guilty about it because it was not his fault that he broke her leg; instead, the fault lies with the man who tripped him. Ted agrees, as he should. He reports that he still feels terrible about breaking the baby's leg. And I reply that this is understandable, given what just happened.

In the memory version of *One Bad Day*, Sally's feeling terrible about killing George would be entirely understandable. But, if I am right, it is not her fault that she killed George. Instead, the fault lies with the manipulators. And because it is not her fault, she should not feel guilty about it and should not regard herself as morally responsible for the killing.

While I am at it, I comment on another worry. On a few occasions, I have heard that I should consider scrapping *One Bad Day* because the radical change in Sally would be so unsettling to her that she would not be able to do much of anything. To be sure, it may be reasonable to expect radical manipulation of the sort featured in that story to have this result, and the story obviously is psychologically unrealistic. However, if it is a conceptually possible story, it is eligible for use as a counterexample to a conceptual claim. The assertion that the change in Sally would *necessarily* be so unsettling to her that she would not kill George is directly relevant to the issue of eligibility, but I know of no promising argument for that bold assertion. *One Bad Day* remains on the table.

I close this section by noting that Frankfurt's own proposed set of sufficient conditions for moral responsibility for an action is not the main issue in this chapter. As I see it, *any* view that renders the symmetrical pair of verdicts about Chuck and Sally that his view renders is false. Now, it may be that what I regard as relatively pure intuitions of mine about moral responsibility in my stories about Chuck and Sally are biased by my commitment to some unacceptable theory or other, or are heavily influenced by my misunderstanding of the true nature of moral responsibility, or the like. In this connection, I do no more *for now* than invite readers who have not already done so to make an honest judgment about whether Chuck and Sally are morally responsible for the killings in my stories about them. (As always, my use of "morally responsible" is the use described in Chapter 1, Section1.)[10]

3. MORE ON CHUCK AND SALLY

So far, I have focused on internal conditions of agents who may be unable to do otherwise than *A* in the circumstances that obtain at the time of action (more on this in Chapter 3). It is time to branch out.

Consider a variant of my story about Chuck in which he has not quite completed his heart-hardening project (see Mele 2009a,

p. 168). He is considering killing Don just for the fun of it, but his internal condition, including his collection of values, is such that he is able to show mercy at the time (at least in some respectable compatibilist sense of "able"), partly in response to an apprehension of some relevant moral reasons that have very little traction with him. Even so, Chuck decides to kill Don, and he succeeds. Call this story *Bad Chuck*.

In a companion story about Sally, manipulators turn her overnight into a partial value twin of the present version of Chuck. She is considering killing George just for the fun of it. Her internal condition, including her collection of values, is such that she is able to show mercy at the time, partly in response to an apprehension of some relevant moral reasons that have very little traction with her. These abilities are not rooted in any preexisting values that survive the change in her. Instead, they are rooted in an implanted collection of values that matches the values in which Chuck's parallel abilities are rooted. Sally decides to kill George, and she succeeds. Call this story *Bad Day Modified*.

In the absence of further details that would get Chuck off the hook, I see him as morally responsible for killing Don. However, I am not the least bit inclined to judge that Sally is morally responsible for killing George. To me, it seems clear that she is *not* morally blameworthy for the killing. If that is right, then given my announced use of "morally responsible," she is not morally responsible for the killing. I believe that the great majority of readers (who do not misread the story) would agree. If it were part of the story that in virtue of her continued possession of some of her pre-manipulation values, Sally was able to conquer her desire to kill George and show mercy, I would not have the belief I just reported. But, again, no surviving pre-transformation values of hers make any contribution to Sally's ability to show mercy.[11] (On nonspecialists' reactions to a toned-down version of *Bad Day Modified*, see the Appendix.)

Intuitions about stories are treated as data for use in the project of conceptual, metaphysical, or linguistic analysis.[12] Of course, because data can be produced in unreliable ways, they should not be accepted uncritically. If Sally is not morally responsible for killing George in *Bad Day Modified,* why not? Exploring this question will prove useful in testing my intuition about her.

It might be suggested that Sally is not morally responsible for killing George because she is not morally responsible for being in the internal condition that issues in her decision to kill him and in her executing that decision. This suggestion (to which I return in Section 4) ignores something interesting. Most lay readers of Sally's story would suppose that pre-manipulation Sally was morally responsible for some of what she did and, at least to a significant extent, for having the character—or collection of values—she had.[13] I suppose this too. Indeed, I make this a feature of the story. Given this feature, a more interesting and attractive suggestion is ready to hand: Sally's pre-transformation character was sufficiently good that killing George was *not even an option for her*; and the combination of this fact with the fact that Sally was morally responsible (to some significant extent) for that character, facts about her history that account for her moral responsibility for that character, facts about her post-manipulation values and associated abilities, and the facts that account for her killing George suffices for her not being morally responsible for killing him. When I ask myself why my gut reaction to Sally's story (insofar as I can have a gut reaction to it) is what it is, these are the considerations that loom large. I dub the suggestion just floated a *radical reversal* suggestion. Similar suggestions about other stories are forthcoming, and the general idea underlying these suggestions is more fully articulated in subsequent chapters. (My suggestion about Sally obviously is about sufficient conditions for her not being morally responsible for killing George. The suggestion makes no claims about whether any of the components is a necessary condition for her not being morally responsible for killing him.)

Substitute the sweetest person you know for Sally in either of my stories about her. (In my case, my dear departed maternal grandmother comes to mind.) If you knew that owing to sudden, radical manipulation of the kind Sally underwent, this person awoke to stalk and kill a neighbor, would you judge that she or he was morally blameworthy for the killing? I doubt it. Replace the manipulators with a bizarre brain tumor that has the same effect on this person.[14] My bet is that this would not change your judgment. Imagine, for good measure, that immediately after the killing, the effects of the manipulation or the tumor are undone: The sweetest person you know is back to normal and has no memory of the gruesome deed.

Is Sally's not being morally responsible for killing George consistent with the truth of compatibilism? The question applies to both of my stories about her, *One Bad Day* and *Bad Day Modified*. Richard Double contends that "the internalistic view is implicit in compatibilism" and "compatibilism has not a chance of plausibility without [internalism], since otherwise the incompatibilist abhorrence of determinism will destroy it" (1991, pp. 56–57). The apparent problem is that one who grants that agents' histories have a bearing of the sort I have been discussing on their moral responsibility for their actions (or on whether they act freely) must also grant that agents' having *deterministic* histories bear on this too, and in a way that undermines compatibilism. (There is a hint of this idea in a sentence from Frankfurt 2002 [p. 28] discussed earlier: "We are inevitably fashioned and sustained, after all, by circumstances over which we have no control." Of course, circumstances over which we have no control influence us even if our universe is not deterministic.)

Two points should be made now.[15] First, *unconditional* internalism definitely is not "implicit in compatibilism." Suppose that my stories about the two drunk drivers are set in a deterministic world.

Compatibilists can maintain—consistently with their compatibilism—that whereas Van is morally responsible for his deterministically caused killing of a pedestrian, Ike is *not* morally responsible for his own deterministically caused killing of a pedestrian. Compatibilists have a long tradition of distinguishing deterministic causation of actions, which they argue to be compatible with moral responsibility for actions, from, for example, compulsion of actions.[16] If determinism is true, the last time I washed my hands, that action of mine was deterministically caused. The same is true of Harvey, a compulsive hand washer. But, according to a familiar compatibilist view, there is a difference in how our respective actions were deterministically caused in virtue of which only one of us—me—washed his hands freely (and was morally responsible for doing so, if the action had some moral significance). Compatibilists can take the same kind of view—with no less plausibility—of, for example, the deterministic causation of the killings mentioned in *Thoroughly Bad Chuck* and *One Bad Day*, assuming now that those stories take place in deterministic worlds. They can consistently contend that Chuck's deterministically caused killing of Don is a free action for which Chuck is morally responsible whereas Sally's deterministically caused killing of George is an unfree action for which she is not morally responsible. Accordingly—and this is my second point—they can consistently reject at least some *conditional* internalist theses: for example, Frankfurt's.

The general idea is that whereas some deterministic causal routes to actions preclude the agents' being morally responsible for the actions, others do not. Even if no general principle has yet been proposed that reliably sorts all possible deterministic routes to action into those that preclude moral responsibility and those that do not, any competent compatibilist will claim that *some but not all* deterministic causal routes to action preclude moral responsibility. If I am right about my two Chuck/Sally pairs, compatibilists should claim—as they can claim consistently with compatibilism (an issue to which

I return in Chapter 4)—that, in a deterministic world, Sally's killing of George (in either story) is deterministically caused in such a way as to preclude her being morally responsible for it, whereas the way in which Chuck's killings are deterministically caused in the same world does *not* preclude his being morally responsible for them.

The direction of value transformation in Sally's stories is good to bad. A story with the opposite direction should also be considered. Here is a quick way to generate such a story. First, add to my story about pre-transformation Sally the detail that she is an extremely generous person who for years has devoted a great deal of time and energy to helping needy people in her community and the local Girl Scouts. Her system of values plays a major role in generating her generous behavior, of course. Second, add to my first story about Chuck the detail that in hardening his heart as he did, he ensured that he had no values at all that could motivate a charitable deed. To be sure, he might buy some Girl Scout cookies to lure an innocent child away for evil purposes; but a cookie-buying motivated in that way is not a charitable deed. Third, bring in the manipulators. Overnight, without Chuck's consent, they erase his bad values and replace them with good ones that match Sally's. Shortly after he awakes, he starts working with a local Habitat for Humanity crew in his neighborhood. When the workday ends, he drives around town for an hour and buys several boxes of Girl Scout cookies from every Girl Scout he sees—about fifty boxes in all. Then he delivers the cookies to a local homeless shelter. His motives are pure, as Sally's are when she does her charitable deeds. When Chuck falls asleep that night, the brainwashing is undone and Chuck returns to normal (for him); the manipulators were conducting a one-day experiment. Call this story *One Good Day*.

I find that I have no inclination at all to believe that Chuck deserves moral credit for the good deeds I described. Most people who see him in action and know nothing of his history would take him to be morally responsible both for his good deeds and for his character. But knowing what I do about his history, I take a very different view of Chuck's deeds and character. (On nonspecialists' reactions to a version of *One Good Day*, see the Appendix.)

Different people sometimes offer opposing verdicts about the same case. When that happens, they might just agree to disagree, but often there is room for discussion and progress. One discussant may be able to show another that the latter's verdict is strongly influenced by, for example, an unfounded worry about implications of the opposing verdict. I explore such matters elsewhere in connection with a story like *One Good Day* and related stories (Mele 1995, pp. 164–73; also see Mele 2006, chap. 7). The following section bears on this issue while avoiding unnecessary repetition of arguments I have offered in previous books.

4. YOUNG AGENTS, INSTANT AGENTS, AND MANIPULATED AGENTS

Consider a generalized and refined version of an idea that I mentioned in Section 3: (*G*) If an agent is not morally responsible for any part or property of the internal condition that issued in his *A*-ing, then he is not morally responsible for *A*. *G* may tempt a theorist seeking to develop an externalist theory of moral responsibility for actions. But if *G* were true, how could a child perform the first (overt or mental) action for which he has some moral responsibility?[17] How is an agent to be morally responsible for a part or property of his internal condition at a time unless he is morally responsible for some *action* of his that helped to produce that condition or that somehow makes him responsible for (some part or property of) that condition? The latter question—which is not a rhetorical one—should have a familiar ring to readers familiar with Galen Strawson's infinite-regress argument for the impossibility of moral responsibility (1986, pp. 28–29).[18] (For a reply, see Mele 1995, pp. 222–30.) Assent to *G* threatens to generate serious problems for believers in morally responsible human beings. And notice that *G* is not entailed by my radical reversal suggestion. Later, I will explain why *G* is interesting in connection with a very special kind of agent.

Return to Sally. One way a theorist might to try to test what kind of role her history should play in an attempt to justify the claim that she is not morally responsible for killing George (both in *One Bad Day* and in *Bad Day Modified*) begins with a story about a special kind of value twin of the very recently transformed Sally—one who just now began to exist (see McKenna 2004, 2012, 2016). In Mele 1995, I discussed an agent with no past "who magically comes into existence with a wealth of beliefs, desires, and values in place" (p. 172). Even if such agents are possible, an agent of the sort at issue may be so foreign to any ordinary conception of morally responsible agency that many readers who keep the detail that the agent has just now begun to exist squarely in mind may have no intuitions—or only weak intuitions—about whether, in a story in which such an agent intentionally does someone great harm, he is morally responsible for the featured action. Furthermore, even if some readers have strong intuitions about this, those intuitions may be far from reliable, owing at least partly to the particular gulf between the imagined agent and any actual agents they have ever deemed morally responsible for an action.

That having been said, four brief stories about an agent with no agential past—an *instant agent*—may be considered. Two of the stories feature a value twin of the first Chuck. One is produced by a supernatural being whose aim is to create an agent who will kill George very soon, and the other is produced by blind forces (a lightning bolt hits a swamp and a fully formed agent emerges from the muck).[19] The remaining two stories are about value twins of the second Chuck—the one who had not quite completed his heart-hardening project. One is produced by a supernatural being with the nasty aim I mentioned and the other by blind forces. All four agents are called Betty, all of the Bettys kill George in the first half-hour of their lives, and all of them understand that killing him is morally wrong (as Chuck and Sally understand that their killings are morally wrong). What intuitions do you have about whether these Bettys are morally responsible for killing George?

If your intuition about some or all of the Bettys is that they are morally responsible for killing George (even if you see them as significantly less responsible than Chuck is for a comparable killing) and you share my intuition that their counterpart, Sally in *One Bad Day* and *Bad Day Modified*, is not morally responsible for killing George, that is evidence that historical considerations of the sort my radical reversal suggestion highlights have a grip on you. The same may be true if you have a weak intuition that some (or all) of the Bettys are *not* morally responsible for the killings—or have no intuition about the moral responsibility of (some of) the Bettys for these deeds—and a strong intuition that Sally (in one story or both stories) is not morally responsible for killing George. But, for the reasons I mentioned, I do not place much weight on intuitions about the moral responsibility of instant agents.

Imagine someone telling you that until your seventh—or third, fifth, tenth, or twentieth—birthday, you had no moral responsibility at all for anything you did and that, sometime around noon on that day, you performed an action for which you had unqualified, full-blown moral responsibility. The speaker adds that, from that point on, you normally had such responsibility for morally significant actions of yours. You would probably find these claims laughable. If you and I are agents with full-blown moral responsibility for some of what we do, somehow we gradually grew into that condition. Plainly, as neonates we were not morally responsible for anything, and the people who helped us get beyond infancy and childhood also helped us learn—gradually—how to be morally responsible agents. (That, presumably, is part of the function of moral education.) It is commonly granted that moral responsibility comes in degrees; and if there are human beings with full-blown moral responsibility for some of their actions, it is a good bet that they were morally responsible to a lesser degree for the earliest actions for which they had some moral responsibility.

This difference between us and my instant-agent killers may help to explain why some readers find it difficult to make judgments about the moral responsibility of those agents for their killings. If they have full-blown moral responsibility for any of their deeds, they had the wherewithal for such responsibility from the moment they came into existence. Obviously, they had no learning history—and no past existence at all—at that point.

A salient difference between instant agents and such victims of manipulation as Sally and Chuck in *One Bad Day, Bad Day Modified,* and *One Good Day* is that the latter two agents, at least partly by way of actions for which they were (by hypothesis) morally responsible, had formed full-blown, persisting moral personalities that their manipulators (or blind forces, in alternative scenarios) then suddenly replaced with radically opposed moral personalities. Sally and Chuck—and here, of course, I am writing about these two people, not the "moral personalities"—persist through the internal transformation.[20] Instant agents, if they are possible, come into being equipped with full-blown moral personalities (or, if you like, "practical identities"; see Watson 1996, pp. 231–34).

Return to *G*, which I earlier set aside on grounds having to do with the first actions for which actual agents have some moral responsibility. In this connection, I mentioned Galen Strawson's infinite-regress argument for the impossibility of moral responsibility. He describes "true" or "real" moral responsibility as "*heaven-and-hell* responsibility," a kind of responsibility such that, if we have it, "it makes sense to propose that it could be just—without any qualification—to punish some of us with (possibly everlasting) torment in hell and reward others with (possibly everlasting) bliss in heaven" (2002, p. 451). Readers who are unwilling to go as far as Strawson on the nature of full-blown moral responsibility—that is, all the way to heaven and hell—are still in a position to distinguish full-blown moral responsibility from, for example, mitigated moral responsibility and the moral responsibility of young children. The following variant of *G* is far from obviously false, and it applies to instant agents: (*G**) If an agent has *no moral responsibility at all* for any part or property of the internal condition that issued in his *A*-ing, then he lacks *full-blown moral responsibility* for *A*. (Recall that I take deliberating and deciding to do something to be mental actions. "*A*" here is not limited to overt actions, that is, actions essentially involving peripheral bodily motion.)

As I observed elsewhere:

> Views according to which agents' past decisions can contribute to their moral responsibility for their present decisions naturally lead us to wonder about the earliest decisions for which agents are morally responsible. When we do wonder about that, we need to keep firmly in mind how young these agents may be and how trivial their good and bad deeds may be by comparison with the full range of good and bad adult deeds. [Little] Tony's making the right or the wrong decision about [whether to snatch his younger sister's] toy is not that big a deal, and that is something for theorists to bear in mind when trying to come to a judgment about whether Tony is morally responsible for his decision. (Mele 2006, pp. 130–31)

I added that if, when pondering whether a little decision maker can make a first decision for which he has some moral responsibility, a theorist is focusing on heaven-and-hell responsibility or even simply on scenarios in which adults make decisions that they should expect to have morally serious consequences, certain theoretical problems will loom large. Typical stories about instant agents combine elements of little Tony's story—a story about what may be the first decision for which a young child has any moral responsibility at all—with elements of stories about extreme adult behavior. This strange combination may make it difficult for some readers to have intuitions about whether or not the instant agents in these stories are morally responsible for their featured actions.

Another strategy someone might use to test ways in which facts about Sally's history in my stories about her may bear on the question of whether she is morally responsible for killing George features a significant reduction in the magnitude of the manipulation. Consider another version of Sally's story in which manipulators want to give her a medium-strength urge to kill George because they wonder how she would respond to such an urge. They discover that her collection of values precludes her having an urge to kill anyone: That collection is such that, as long as it persists, her having an urge with that content is not a psychological possibility for her.[21] She is simply way too nice a person to have an urge with that content. So they decide to alter her values. Because operating their machinery is expensive and the cost increases sharply as the magnitude of the manipulation increases, they decide to do just enough value engineering to make it possible for them to induce in Sally a medium-strength urge to kill George and then to induce the urge. Their first few attempts fail: More engineering needs to be done. Eventually they succeed.

To make it easier to keep track of the Sallys, I call the one in this new story Sally*. Although the implanted urge is far from overpowering, Sally* acts on it. Within thirty minutes, she has worked out a plan for killing George. Shortly thereafter, she executes the plan—and George. This part of the story is not easy to accept, of course.

Given the values she had until the manipulation and the fact that only enough engineering was done to enable the manipulators to implant the medium-strength urge, why would Sally* act on it? Why wouldn't she conquer it—perhaps after seeking psychiatric help? With these questions left unanswered, I find that I do not understand Sally*'s story well enough to have an intuition about whether she is morally responsible for the killing. Different answers to them may generate different intuitions.

The following story is much easier to comprehend. Three months ago, Carl resolved not to eat any snacks for six months, mainly to address his weight problem but also to test his willpower. On average, Carl—who has not yet been manipulated—has a couple of medium-strength urges for a snack per day. On about one day in ten, he acts on such an urge; usually, he successfully resists these urges. Just for the fun of it, a manipulator flashes a subliminal message at Carl that he knows will give him a medium-strength urge for a snack. Carl succumbs to the urge. Over the next three months, the manipulator tries his trick once each day; and Carl succumbs about 5% of the time.

When Carl acts on a medium-strength urge produced by such manipulation, is he morally responsible for eating the snack? Provided that he is morally responsible for eating snacks when the medium-strength urges at work are not produced by manipulation, a plausible answer is *yes*. The difference between a medium-strength urge's being produced by manipulation and such an urge's being produced in a "normal" way that involves no other agent may well have a bearing on moral responsibility. The *manipulator* may have some moral responsibility for Carl's eating the snack. But that is compatible with Carl's also being morally responsible for eating it. Consider a related scenario. A mischievous acquaintance, Ali, enjoys tempting Carl to eat snacks. She tempts him by bringing his favorite snacks to his office around mid-afternoon, eating one—with an obvious display of pleasure—while chatting with him, and offering him another. If Ali manages to produce a medium-strength urge for a snack in Carl and he succumbs to it, she may well have some moral responsibility for Carl's eating the snack; but so does Carl, other things being equal. Given that Carl is able to refrain from acting on medium-strength urges to eat snacks and has a pretty impressive record of successfully resisting such urges, his being morally responsible for eating snacks in response to such urges is implausibly regarded as turning on whether the urges are produced, on the one hand, in the "normal" way or by Ali's antics or, on the other, by a manipulator who flashes subliminal "snack" messages at him. By hypothesis, the difference in sources has no effect on the resistibility of the medium-strength urges; and, of course, Ali too is manipulating Carl.

Readers who agree that, with the proviso I identified, Carl is morally responsible for eating snacks when the medium-strength urges to which he succumbs are produced by subliminal manipulation and who also agree with me that Sally, in *One Bad Day* and *Bad Day Modified*, is not morally responsible for killing George probably experience no cognitive dissonance. (I am setting Sally* aside.) There are clear differences between Sally and Carl that promise to be useful in accounting for the asymmetrical judgments. Sally's pre-transformation character was sufficiently good that killing George was not even an option for her, whereas Carl's pre-manipulation character definitely did not render eating snacks a non-option for him. Although Carl's manipulation is limited to the production of urges of a kind that he often acquires in the absence of any monkey business, Sally's system of values was turned upside down.

How far-reaching is a correct externalist view of moral responsibility for actions? A thorough defense of a detailed answer to this question requires careful attention to a wide range of cases. There are lots of variables to tweak, including the moral personalities of agents prior to manipulation, the extent to which these agents are morally responsible for those personalities, the depth and breadth of the manipulation, whether the manipulation is reversible by the agent and, if so, how difficult it would be for the agent to reverse it, and how bad or good the post-manipulation actions are. Another item up for tweaking is whether the world in which a story is set is deterministic or indeterministic. (For some manipulation stories explicitly set in indeterministic worlds, see Mele 2006, pp. 139–44. Some stories of this kind are discussed in subsequent chapters.) A full defense of a detailed answer to my question about far-reachingness would be a major undertaking. This book takes us part of the way.

I have suggested that a correct view of moral responsibility for actions will render the verdicts that Ike (the drunk driver who was force-fed alcohol), the manipulated Sallys (which group does not include Sally*), and Chuck in *One Good Day* are not morally responsible for their featured actions. I have also observed that the subliminal manipulation in Carl's case does not get him off the hook for succumbing to his medium-strength urge to eat a snack. I suspect that any serious attempt to sort actions into those for which their agents are morally responsible and those for which this is not so will turn up significant vagueness. How much further in its nonresponsibility verdicts a correct externalism will go beyond the verdicts I claimed it yields about Ike, the brainwashed Sallys, and brainwashed Chuck I cannot now say. But I can say that it will not go so far as to let Carl off the hook. My main aim in this chapter has been to lay some groundwork for productive explorations of the place of agents' histories in promising theories or analyses of moral responsibility for actions and to begin motivating a conditional externalist view. I have attended to some stories that may not generate intuitions at all in many readers or may generate intuitions of highly questionable value. One purpose I had for so doing was to identify some potential pitfalls for theorists seeking an account of moral responsibility. I return to instant agents and related matters in Chapter 3.

I observed that conditional internalism is compatible with *conditional externalism*—the thesis that even if some conditional internalist thesis is true, agents sometimes are morally responsible for *A* partly because of how they came to be in the internal condition that issues in their *A*-ing; and, more specifically, in these cases, there is another possible way of having come to be in that internal condition such that if they had come to be in that condition in that way, then, holding everything else fixed (except what is entailed by the difference), including the fact that they *A*-ed, they would not have been morally responsible for *A*. If it is assumed that Van, unmanipulated Chuck, and unmanipulated Sally are morally responsible for their featured deeds in my stories about them, then, if my verdicts about any of drunk Ike, *One Bad Day, Bad Day Modified,* and *One Good Day* are correct, conditional externalism is true. A conditional externalism that takes us no further than comparative judgments about Van and Ike take us is not especially impressive. But I have moved beyond such a restricted conditional externalism already, and there is more to come.

In Chapter 1, I asked readers to imagine that they have decided to construct an analysis of "*S* is morally responsible for *A*-ing," where *S* is a placeholder for any possible agent and *A* is a placeholder for any possible action. Suppose that all of the verdicts mentioned in the preceding paragraph are correct and that the unmanipulated counterparts of these agents are morally responsible for the deeds at issue. Then reference to agents' histories will enter into any adequate *analysis* of moral responsibility. Such reference will be needed, for example, to yield the result that even though unmanipulated Sally is morally responsible for helping the Girl Scouts, Chuck is not morally responsible for doing this in *One Good Day*.[22]

Chapter 3

Instant Agents, Minutelings, and Radical Reversals

More than twenty years ago, I told a tale about a pair of philosophers, Ann and Beth (1995, pp. 145–46). Some people seem fond of this duo; at any rate, the tale has received a lot of attention. In a relatively recent article making a case for the thesis that "nonhistorical" compatibilism—that is, *internalist* compatibilism, in my terminology—is not dead yet, Michael McKenna brings Ann and Beth back to the stage (2012). Here, after a brief review of my story about them and some related matters, I take up some of the interesting questions about moral responsibility, free will, and manipulation raised in McKenna 2012. I then turn to some related issues raised by Manuel Vargas (2006, 2013). My critical discussion of their work reinforces the externalist position defended in this book. I wrap up the chapter by illustrating how ignoring radical reversal stories (which McKenna and Vargas do not do) can lead one astray.

1. SETTING THE STAGE

Here is a short version of the tale of Ann and Beth. In the absence of any serious monkey business, Ann gradually became an extremely hard-working philosopher who loves her work while her colleague Beth developed into an easygoing person who spends much less time on philosophy and enjoys a wide variety of pleasant pursuits. Both are reflective people who have reflectively endorsed their lifestyles and their associated values. One day, their dean decides to turn Beth into a hard-working philosopher like Ann by means of heavy-duty brainwashing. The brainwashers instill pertinent parts of Ann's system of values in Beth overnight while eradicating all competing values. The next day, Beth is surprised by the change. Her "hypothesis is that she simply has grown tired of her previous mode of life, that her life had become stale without her recognizing it, and that she finally has come fully to appreciate the value of philosophical work. When she carefully reflects on her preferences and values, Beth finds that they fully support a life dedicated to philosophical work, and she wholeheartedly embraces such a life and the collection of values that supports it" (Mele 1995, p. 145).

I used the story to set up a discussion of what I called "psychological autonomy" and especially the autonomous possession of a value over a stretch of time. As I pointed out, "to the extent to which one can successfully counteract the influence of brainwashing, having been a victim of that form of 'mind control' does not necessarily render one nonautonomous" regarding the continued possession of values produced by brainwashing (Mele 1995, p. 148). I also observed that "any process of critical reflection is conducted, at any given time, from some perspective or other. If the perspective from which an agent critically reflects upon his 'first-order preferences and desires' [Dworkin 1988, p. 108] at a time is dominated by values produced by brainwashing, and dominated in such a way as to dictate the results of his critical reflection, it is difficult to view the reflection as autonomously conducted and the results as autonomously produced. There is at least a worry here that requires attention" (pp. 147–48).

With this worry in mind, I developed a notion of "unsheddable values." I described my simple conception of values and valuing in Chapter 1: Briefly, valuing *X* is believing *X* to be good while also desiring *X*; and when values are understood as psychological states, they are such belief-desire pairs. One may shed a value either by eradicating it or by significantly attenuating it. Sometimes, we can persuade ourselves that something we have believed for some time to be good in fact is not good. In this way, we can eradicate a value of ours (provided that the eradicated belief had been paired with a corresponding desire). We can also significantly diminish the strength of some of our desires by means of reflection or various strategies of self-control discussed earlier in Mele 1995 (chaps. 1–3). If we do this to a desire we have for *X* that is paired with a belief that *X* is good, we have attenuated the pertinent value. If we manage to extinguish such a desire, we have eradicated the value.

I made a case for the claim that given how deeply entrenched some values are, the person's shedding them in the circumstances he occupies over, say, "a two-week span . . . is not a psychologically genuine option" (Mele 1995, p. 153). My primary example featured the parental values of a man named Al. After sketching a story about his acquisition of those values through a voluntary program of self-improvement, I added:

> Of course, there might be conditions beyond Al's control such that, were they to arise, he would shed these values. He might become hopelessly insane, for example. Or CIA agents might use Al's parental values as a lever to motivate him to uproot those very values: they might convince him that the CIA will ensure his children's flourishing if he uproots his parental values and that, otherwise, they will destroy his children's lives. Under these conditions (I will suppose), Al would take himself to have a decisive reason for shedding his parental values; and if he thought

> hard enough, he might find a way to shed them. (Once he sheds the values, he might not care at all how his children fare; but that is another matter.) However, if, in fact, conditions such as these do not arise for Al in the next two weeks, neither will he shed his parental values during that period. Insofar as (1) the conditions that would empower Al to shed these values are "beyond his control"—that is, insofar as his psychological constitution precludes his voluntarily producing those conditions—and (2) the obtaining of those conditions independently of Al's voluntarily producing them is not in the cards, he is apparently stuck with the values. (p. 153)

My next two sentences were these: "I will say that any agent who is stuck in this way with a value (during *t*) is *practically unable* to shed it (during *t*). Values that one is practically unable to shed may be termed *practically unsheddable*" (Mele 1995, p. 153). And I went on to say that "The notion of ability at work here is similar to one implicit in commonsense conceptions of irresistible desires" (p. 154). As I understand irresistible desires, a desire might be irresistible by an agent even if there are extreme counterfactual scenarios in which he resists it.[1] Analogously, someone who is not in a position, over a two-week span, to eradicate or attenuate a value by means of reflection or the various relevant strategies for self-control available to him—someone for whom that value is practically unsheddable over that span of time—may be able to do this in extreme counterfactual scenarios during that span of time. Part of my aim in selecting a two-week span for my illustration, rather than, for example, a brief period of deliberation, was to reinforce the idea that practically unsheddable values—*unsheddable values,* for short—run deep. Values that one cannot shed in a few minutes may be sufficiently malleable for one to shed under ordinary circumstances in an hour. An hour of careful reflection may be enough to disabuse oneself of an unwarranted belief that something is good, and an hour of sustained effort to weaken a desire by employing a self-control technique one has learned may suffice to weaken it significantly. But unsheddable values, as I understand them, are much more resistant to significant change than that. Setting aside science fiction, magical powers, and the like, they run much too deep to be eradicated or significantly attenuated by means of an hour's hard work. In any case, my main point now is that unsheddable values are supposed to be very firmly entrenched parts of the valuer's psyche.

After various twists and turns, I offered a sufficient condition for its being false that a person with an unsheddable pro-attitude over a span of time is compelled to possess it over that span and a sufficient condition for its being true that a person with such a pro-attitude is "compelled*" to possess it (over a span of time). As I understand the pertinent terms, our values count as pro-attitudes. One feature of compulsion* is that the compulsion is not arranged by the compelled agent (Mele 1995, p. 166). For another feature, see 2* in the following list. Here are the two sufficient conditions I mentioned:

1. Barring compelled "innate" pro-attitudes, an agent who is practically unable (over a span of time) to shed a pro-attitude *P* with which he strongly identifies for reasons whose possession is *not* explained by a bypassing of his capacities for control over his mental life is *not* compelled to possess *P*. (p. 171)

2*. If an agent *S* comes to possess a pro-attitude *P* in a way that bypasses *S*'s (perhaps relatively modest) capacities for control over his mental life; and the bypassing issues in *S*'s being practically unable to shed *P*; and the bypassing was not itself arranged (or performed) by *S*; and *S* neither presently possesses nor earlier possessed pro-attitudes that would support his identifying with *P*, with the exception of pro-attitudes that are themselves

> practically unsheddable products of unsolicited bypassing; then *S* is compelled* to possess *P*. (p. 172)

Technical terminology in 1 and 2* that I have not yet discussed requires brief attention. In Mele 1995 (pp. 166–72, 183–84), I argued for the relevance of a notion of agents' capacities for control over their mental lives being *bypassed*. In ideally self-controlled agents (see pp. 121–22), these capacities are impressive. Such agents are capable of modifying the strengths of their desires in the service of their normative judgments, of bringing their emotions into line with relevant judgments, and of mastering motivation that threatens (sometimes via the biasing of practical or theoretical reasoning) to produce or sustain beliefs in ways that would violate their principles for belief-acquisition and belief-retention. They also are capable of rationally assessing their values and principles; of identifying with their values and principles on the basis of informed, critical reflection; and of modifying their values and principles should they judge that to be in order. Most readers of this book have each of these capacities in some measure. All such capacities—including modest ones possessed by agents who fall well short of ideal self-control—are bypassed in the induction (and erasing) of values in cases of value engineering of the sort at issue. In such cases, new values are not generated via an exercise or an activation of agents' capacities for control over their mental lives; rather, they are generated despite the agents' capacities for this. The agents are compelled to acquire these values and compelled to possess them for some time.

The following passage from Mele 2006 collects some examples of exercises of capacities for control over one's mental life:

> Sometimes we are told that, or wonder whether, we care too much—or too little—about our work, what others think of us, our children's success, how we dress, money, our health, or

> whatever. Sometimes, on reflection, we judge that we should care less—or more—about some of these things. Occasionally we make efforts to get ourselves to care less—or more. Someone who becomes convinced that he cares way too little about his health may try to get himself to care much more by spending time each day picturing opportunities that would be closed to him by poor health and thinking about the ways in which better health would improve his life, someone who judges that he cares way too much about work may attempt to fix that by reflecting periodically on the good things that his work leaves him little time for, and so on. Sometimes such efforts are successful, and no such effort would succeed if the values at issue were unsheddable (at the time). [Values that] are revisable in this way . . . differ from unsheddable values that some workaholics, misers, and health fanatics may have. How, exactly, the distinction is spelled out by a particular compatibilist depends on that theorist's preferred way of understanding what it is to have been able, in deterministic worlds, to do things that one did not do. I leave that open. (Mele 2006, p. 186)

The capacities exercised in these examples are among the agential capacities bypassed in my stories about heavy-duty manipulation (such stories as *One Good Day, One Bad Day*, and *Bad Day Modified*).

I introduced the notion of *innate* pro-attitudes in connection with magically produced agents of a certain kind (Mele 1995, p. 168). Suppose a supernatural being can create an agent with some unsheddable pro-attitudes, "identifications," and reasons for identification already in place at the time of creation. In producing these items, the creator does not "bypass" the agent's capacities for control over his mental life; for the agent has no such capacities when the items are produced. Still, the agent is reasonably viewed as being possessed of some *compelled* pro-attitudes with which he identifies (for reasons). I called such attitudes compelled *innate* pro-attitudes. And I added that the notion of innate pro-attitudes may be extended to apply to beings who, after coming into existence, but prior to having any (relevant) capacities for control over their mental lives, are subjected to pro-attitude engineering.

As I pointed out in Mele 1995, the historical constraint that I argued for on "the autonomous possession of values and other pro-attitudes (i.e., on *P*-autonomy) is a *negative* one. My claim is not that *P*-autonomy regarding a pro-attitude, *P*, requires that the agent *have* a history of a certain kind, but rather that he *lack* a certain kind of history—a history yielding what I have called 'compulsion*' of *P*" (p. 172). Another magical agent helps explain why. Athena "magically comes into existence with a wealth of beliefs, desires, and values in place" (p. 172). And "she has a robust ability to shed each of her pro-attitudes—an analogue of the ability that we have to refrain from acting on resistible desires" (p. 173). "Other things being equal," I wrote, "there is no bar to Athena's autonomously possessing her pro-attitudes." If Athena is a possible being and if her value-shedding ability is such that she can shed values instantaneously, she may autonomously possess values throughout a stretch of time that begins when she begins to exist. Obviously, when she comes into existence, she has no history as an agent.

The focus of the discussion in Mele 1995 of the importance of history for a plausible compatibilism is what I call "psychological autonomy," especially the autonomous possession of particular values over a stretch of time and autonomous deliberation. My view is that compatibilists about autonomy, including autonomous action, would accomplish their main positive task—that is, showing that compatibilism about this is true—"by showing how determinism is compatible with *psychological* autonomy. If [that compatibility] can be demonstrated, compatibilists can rest their case; the possibility of autonomous overt action raises no special worries about determinism beyond those raised by the possibility of psychological autonomy itself" (p. 193). (Here, I am saying that they can rest their case for the truth of *compatibilism* about autonomy. This is not to say that they would not need to bother about any of the other questions about autonomy that may concern a theorist who endorses compatibilism about autonomy: for example, questions about the merits of internalist and externalist views in this sphere.)

I did not develop a general position on conditions under which histories of certain kinds would render it false that specific *overt actions* (that is, as I have mentioned, actions essentially involving peripheral bodily motion) are autonomous, free, or deeds for which their agents are morally responsible. However, as I pointed out elsewhere (Mele 2008, pp. 268–69), if asked, I would have endorsed the following cautious claim, for example:

> *NFM*. An agent who performs an overt action *A* does not freely *A* and is not morally responsible for *A*-ing, if (1) he expresses unsheddable values in *A*-ing; (2) owing directly to those values, he could not have done otherwise than *A* in the circumstances (on a compatibilist reading of "could have done otherwise"); (3) those values were very recently produced in a way that bypassed his capacities for control over his mental life by value engineering to which he did not consent and are seriously at odds with autonomously acquired values of his that were erased in the process; (4) he retains no preexisting value that is promoted by his having the unsheddable values he expresses in *A*-ing; and (5) *A* is the first overt action he performs on the basis of his new values.[2]

The notion at work here of an agent's *expressing* a value in an action has an essential causal dimension. If values are psychological states, then, by definition, an action *A* expresses a value *V* only if *V* (or its neural realizer) plays a nondeviant causal role in the production of *A*. (For a defense of a version of *NFM*, see Mele 2006, chap. 7.)

It turns out that this cautious claim was not cautious enough. Recall pre-manipulation Sally from Chapter 2. Imagine that she knows that there is a 10% chance that manipulators will turn her into a partial value twin of Chuck for a day if she goes out under a full moon. She knows the moon is full tonight, but she sees a kitten wandering in the street in front of her house and, after reflecting on the potential cost to the kitten, to herself, and to anyone she might end up harming if the manipulators get their hands on her, she ventures out to save the kitten, against her better judgment. As a consequence of her being out under a full moon, the manipulators work on her that night. The rest of the story is very similar to *One Bad Day*. Sally kills George early the next day.[3]

It is plausible that Sally is indirectly morally responsible (to some degree) for killing George, despite satisfying *NFM*'s five conditions. Her moral responsibility for killing George would seem to trace back to her moral responsibility for venturing out under a full moon to save the kitten, despite what she knew about the potential consequences. The fix I favor is to add something to condition 3: namely, that the agent has no moral responsibility for the "value engineering." This addition appears later in this chapter in *NFM*'s successor.

2. MCKENNA ON INTERNALISM AND EXTERNALISM

Michael McKenna and I have exchanged ideas in print on the proper place of agents' histories in a plausible compatibilist view of moral responsibility and free will (see McKenna 2004, 2012, 2016, and Mele 2008, 2009b, 2013d). For a variety of reasons, these exchanges have not quite clicked. In the case of McKenna 2012, one reason for the less than ideal clicking involves a bit of technical terminology of mine that I commented on in Section 1—"practically unsheddable values." McKenna writes: "I strongly suspect that most values that most actual persons possess at a time are such that, at that very time, those values are practically unsheddable for them" (2012, p. 148). This is an indication that he and I use my technical term "shed" very differently. And the indication is on target. As McKenna understands value shedding, to be able to shed a value is to be to "be able to lose or substantially downgrade [it] *at will*" (p. 148, my emphasis). (I take it that being able to *A* at will entails being able to *A* very easily and with very little effort. This reading is standard not only in ordinary usage but also in the philosophy of action.)[4] As is clear from my discussion in Section 1, I understand value shedding and the corresponding ability very differently. I agree with McKenna that, in actual people, most values are unsheddable in his sense. In fact, "most" is an understatement. (How frequently do we eradicate beliefs *at will* or significantly reduce or increase the strength of a desire of ours *at will*?) But, as is clear from Section 1, not being sheddable at will is far from sufficient for being unsheddable in my sense. If McKenna had argued that most values are unsheddable given my characterization of unsheddable values, there would be something for us to argue about on the topic of unsheddable values. But, as it stands, he simply uses some technical terminology of mine very differently than I do. More on this later.

McKenna writes: "The interesting philosophical controversy up for dispute, I contend, has to do with whether directly free acts, ones for which an agent is directly morally responsible, are such that a history condition is required for them" (2012, p. 156). A comment on this issue is in order now.

Recall *One Good Day* (Chapter 2). I assume, as I have mentioned, that if a person is morally responsible for a good deed he performs, then he deserves some moral credit for it. As I have reported, I find that I have no inclination at all to believe that Chuck deserves moral credit for his good deeds in *One Good Day*. Suppose that I am right about Chuck and return to unmanipulated Sally (from Chapter 2). If directly free good deeds and good deeds for which agents are directly morally responsible are common in Sally's world, I see no reason to believe that the good deeds Sally performs as an adult that express her admirable moral character are never directly free and never ones for which she is directly morally responsible.[5] (I suggest that direct freedom be understood as follows, by analogy with my gloss on direct moral responsibility in Chapter 1, Section 2: An agent *directly* freely *A*-s when and only when he freely *A*-s and the freedom of his *A*-ing is not wholly inherited from the freedom of other things. Also see McKenna 2012, p. 125, where *indirectly* free actions are characterized as being "such that their status as free is entirely derivative.") For a day, Sally and Chuck are partial value twins (see Chapter 2); but, if I am right, only one of them is morally responsible for deeds motivated by the relevant values on that day and only one of them freely performs those deeds. Moreover, as far as I can see, at least some of Sally's free good deeds are *directly* free and she is *directly* morally responsible for them.

In Chapter 2, I offered what I called a *radical reversal suggestion* about Sally in *Bad Day Modified*. The basic idea, as it applies to *One Good Day*, is that the following collection of facts suffices for Chuck's deserving no moral credit for his good deeds in that story: the fact that his pre-transformation character was sufficiently bad that charitable deeds were *not even an option for him*, the fact that he was morally responsible (to some significant extent) for that character, the facts about his history that account for his moral responsibility for that character, facts about his post-manipulation values and associated abilities, and the facts that account for the good deeds at issue.[6] If it is assumed that a person deserves some moral credit for performing a good deed if he performs it freely, then this radical reversal suggestion has implications for free action as well.

I return to my radical reversal suggestions later in this chapter. In the meantime, I explore the question of how the interesting discussion of instant agents in McKenna 2012 bears on these suggestions and then take up an argument McKenna offers about a positive versus a negative line on the importance of history for the performance of free actions and actions for which one is morally responsible.

Consider the case of Suzie Instant introduced in McKenna 2004 and revisited in McKenna 2012 and 2016. "Suzie Instant is created by a god at an instant and is placed in a determined world. She is created to be a psychologically healthy woman indistinguishable from any other normally functioning thirty-year-old person.... Suzie has some range of unsheddable values. She also has a set of false beliefs about how she came to acquire those values" (McKenna 2012, pp. 160–61). Suzie is reasons-responsive and self-controlled, and, when she acts, "varying compatibilists would regard [her agential properties] as adequate for satisfying all of the nonhistorical conditions highlighted in their respective accounts of CAS [the Compatibilist-friendly Agential Structure]" (p. 161).

Imagine that Suzie Instant is a value twin of Beth in my story about Ann and Beth. McKenna formulates an argument "for treating the cases of Beth and Suzie Instant in the same way" (2012, p. 162):

> Suzie Instant is alleged to be free and morally responsible on compatibilist grounds. Assume she is. If so, it at least *appears* that, solely by virtue of nonhistorical properties just subsequent to her A-ing, she satisfies sufficient conditions for A-ing freely and being responsible for it. But, by hypothesis, Beth satisfies the same nonhistorical properties as does Suzie Instant when Beth A-s. Hence, if Suzie Instant A-s freely and is morally responsible

> for doing so, then Beth A-s freely and is also morally responsible for doing so. If, on the other hand, Beth does not A freely and is not morally responsible, it seems that the same ruling applies to Suzie Instant, since the case of Beth shows that the nonhistorical properties both satisfy are insufficient for acting freely. (2012, pp. 162–63)

Obviously, someone who advocates, as I do, a negative historical constraint on the autonomous possession of values over a stretch of time, might also advocate a negative historical constraint on free action and action that one is morally responsible for performing. Such a person might hold that just as Athena might autonomously possess her initial values for some time, her earliest actions might be free actions and actions for which she is morally responsible. (Recall that Athena "has a robust ability to shed each of her pro-attitudes" [Mele 1995, p. 173].)

McKenna recognizes this. But, he asks (2012, p. 167), "how convincing is a purely negative historical condition?" And he argues that "the motivation for such a thesis falls short." McKenna's argument for this features attention to the following two propositions (p. 167):

> *POS.* An agent A-s freely and is morally responsible for doing so only if, with respect to the causal springs of her A-ing, she has a history that *does not* include the acquisition of any unsheddable values through means that bypassed her ability to critically acquire, assess and sustain them.
>
> *NEG.* An agent A-s freely and is morally responsible for doing so only if, with respect to the causal springs of her A-ing, she *does not* have a history that includes the acquisition of any unsheddable values through means that bypassed her ability to critically acquire, assess and sustain them.

Both *POS* and *NEG* are false. Before I explain why, focusing on just one kind of reason for rejecting both propositions, a comment on Mele 1995 is in order. I suggest there that an agent may come to autonomously possess unsheddable values—in my sense of "unsheddable," of course—that were initially installed in him by brainwashing that bypasses the abilities at issue, and I explain how that can be (Mele 1995 pp. 170–72 and 175–76 n. 30). An agent who does eventually come to possess such values autonomously may act autonomously, freely, and morally responsibly on their basis. But I let this point pass, because I assume we are meant to understand unsheddable values here in McKenna's way. Recall that for a value to be McKenna-unsheddable is for it to be such that the person who has it cannot shed it *at will*.

In a wide range of possible cases of manipulation, values induced in ways that bypass the agent's relevant capacities are such that an agent may freely and morally responsibly act on them. A story I told in Chapter 2 about Carl and an induced medium-strength urge for a snack is relevant here. I modify it a bit to apply directly to McKenna's position. In this version, just for the fun of it, a manipulator flashes a subliminal message at Carl that he knows will give him a medium-strength urge to eat a snack soon *together with a belief that eating one soon would be good*. So he causes Carl to *value* eating a snack soon, in my thin sense of "value," and he does this in a way that bypasses the abilities mentioned in *POS* and *NEG*. Carl acts on that value, and he is not able to shed it at will: It is McKenna-unsheddable. Over the next three months, the manipulator tries his trick once each day; and Carl acts on the resulting McKenna-unsheddable value about 5% of the time.

When Carl acts on a medium-strength, McKenna-unsheddable value produced by such manipulation, is he morally responsible for eating the snack and does he eat it freely? Provided that he is morally responsible for eating snacks and eats them freely when the medium-strength values at work are not produced by manipulation, an extremely plausible answer is *yes*, for the reasons I adduced in my discussion of Carl's case in Chapter 2. Because Carl is able to refrain from acting on medium-strength, McKenna-unsheddable values for snack-eating and has a rather impressive record of successfully resisting such values, his being morally responsible for eating snacks in response to such values and his eating them freely is implausibly regarded as turning on whether the values are produced in the "normal" way or instead by a manipulator who flashes subliminal "snack" messages at him, thereby bypassing the abilities mentioned in *POS* and *NEG*. By hypothesis, the difference in sources has no effect on how easy or difficult it is for Carl to resist the medium-strength, McKenna-unsheddable values. This story about Carl falsifies both *POS* and *NEG*.

McKenna says that he wants "to claim . . . that the plausibility of [*NEG*] rests on the prior plausibility of [*POS*]—not in the sense that [*POS*] is sufficient for [*NEG*], but just in the sense that any motive for embracing [*NEG*] would be lacking if there were not good reason to embrace [*POS*]" (2012, pp. 167–68). Even though both *POS* and *NEG* are false, something in the ballpark of what McKenna says he wants to claim is worth exploring. When it comes to instant agents and non-instant value twins who *A*, might there be relevant cases in which only the instant agent *A*-s freely and only the instant agent is morally responsible for *A*-ing?

It is time to bring a new kind of being on stage—minutelings. Here is the story. Cloned human bodies are kept unconscious for years. Their muscles get a lot of daily exercise as the bodies grow and mature. For each body, a complete psychological profile of some actual human being or other is created, including a whole raft of pseudo-memories that match the human being's actual memories. At a certain point, the body and psychological profile are merged. And now, for the first time, a conscious being is located where the body is.

Given the skills and technology of the people in charge, the being can live no more than a minute.

Let me give you an example. I start with a normal, reasons-responsive human agent whose psychological profile was implanted in a minuteling. Marty, a soldier who sometimes serves on firing lines, has firing-line duty today. Today's target is an innocent political prisoner, as he learned; and he believes that it would be wrong to shoot her. Marty is confident that he can fire into the wall (rather than the prisoner) without anyone knowing. He is confident that at least a few of the other nine shooters on the firing line will shoot the prisoner. As he stands on the firing line with his rifle pointed at the prisoner, about to hear the order to fire, Marty is undecided about what to do.

A minuteling is turned on as his body stands on another firing line. His rifle is pointed at a prisoner. He believes that he has been standing there thinking about what to do for a while, that his name is Marty, that he is a soldier, that the target is an innocent political prisoner, that it would be wrong to shoot her, and so on. He is confident about the same things Marty is and he is undecided about what to do. A few milliseconds later, he hears the command to fire, and he decides to shoot the prisoner. (Marty made the same decision.) Accordingly, he shoots the prisoner. Less than a minute later, he falls over dead (about the same time the prisoner does).

Assume that Marty's agential properties are, in McKenna's words, "adequate for satisfying all of the nonhistorical conditions highlighted in [various compatibilist] accounts of CAS" (p. 161). (CAS, again, is McKenna's acronym for "Compatibilist-friendly Agential Structure" [2012, p. 149].) Perhaps the same is true of the minuteling, despite his false beliefs about himself. (That depends on the details of the proposed CAS at issue.) Question: Does the minuteling freely decide to shoot the prisoner, and is he morally responsible for shooting her? I leave answering this question as an exercise for the reader. I have not said whether the world in which my story is set is deterministic or indeterministic. Readers who think my exercise would be interesting to pursue are encouraged to try it both ways.

Suppose you decide to take up this exercise and you are currently feeling very unsettled about how to answer my question about the minuteling. In that case, it might be wise for you to turn your attention to something else for a while. I invite you to consider another firing-line story. This one involves pre-manipulation Sally, who has not had a violent impulse in a great many years. Last night she was brainwashed, and her relevant values were replaced with values that are almost as bad as pre-transformation Chuck's. Today she was invited to take part in a firing-squad execution, and she accepted. Like Marty and the minuteling, Sally believes that the target is an innocent political prisoner, that it would be wrong to shoot her, and that she can fire into the wall without anyone knowing. As she stands on the firing line, rifle raised, and about to hear the order to fire, Sally is undecided about what to do. But the values of hers that survived the brainwashing—values regarding food and soft drinks, for example—play no role at all in accounting for her indecision. She is undecided because, although she has a strong desire to find out what it would feel like to kill someone, a tiny collection of the implanted values speaks in favor of showing mercy. When she hears the command to fire, Sally decides to shoot the prisoner.

What is your verdict on this case? Is Sally morally responsible for deciding to shoot the prisoner? And does she freely decide to shoot her? My answer to both questions is *no*. And the general idea behind my radical reversal suggestions about earlier stories is relevant to both judgments. Sally's pre-transformation character was sufficiently good that deciding to shoot someone she believed to be innocent was *not even an option for her*; and the combination of this fact with the fact that Sally was morally responsible (to some significant extent) for that character, facts about her history that account for her moral responsibility for that character, facts about her post-manipulation values and associated abilities, and the facts that account for her deciding to shoot the prisoner suffices for her not being morally responsible for deciding to shoot her and for her not freely deciding to do that. When I ask myself why my gut reaction to this new story about Sally (insofar as I can have a gut reaction to it) is what it is, these are the considerations that loom large.

Notice that the collection of facts just cited is far from matched by any collection of facts about the minuteling. Taking the view I do on Sally does not commit me to holding that the minuteling is not morally responsible for deciding to shoot the prisoner and does not freely decide to shoot her. Asymmetrical judgments on these matters regarding Sally and the minuteling are open to me. It also is open to me to take the view I do on Sally while being agnostic about whether the minuteling's decision is free and whether he is morally responsible for it.

McKenna frowns on my having appealed to grandmothers in connection with cases like that of brainwashed Sally (McKenna 2012, p. 165). But I will do it again anyway, as I did in Chapter 2. In Mele 2009a (as in Chapter 2), I invited my readers to substitute for a person like pre-manipulation Sally the sweetest person they know, and I pointed out that, in my case, my maternal grandmother came to mind (p. 169). If you knew that owing to sudden, radical manipulation of the kind Sally underwent, this person decided to shoot someone she or he believed to be an innocent political prisoner, would you judge that she or he was morally blameworthy for that decision? I doubt it. Replace the manipulators with a brain tumor that has the same effect on this person. My bet (as in Chapter 2) is that this would not change your judgment. Imagine, finally, that immediately after the shooting, the effects of the manipulation or the tumor are undone: The sweetest person you know is back to normal and has no memory of what she or he recently did.

In the preceding paragraph I echo invitations and opinions from Mele 2009a (pp. 169–70). Regarding my invitation to imagine the sweetest person one knows, McKenna objects that, "Aside from the emotional noise this can generate as regards reliable intuitive responses, it is also true that for some to whom we are closely connected, we have good reasons not to blame them overtly, *even if they are blameworthy*. Grandmothers seem to me to be good candidates for being in that camp" (2012, p. 165). But I did not ask my readers whether they would blame the person; I asked whether they would judge that the person was morally blameworthy for the deed. I took my audience to be philosophers with an interest in the topic—not people who would take their not feeling like blaming someone or their attitude specifically about their overtly blaming someone to justify the belief that the person is not blameworthy. The invitation to think of the sweetest person one knows is supposed to make an important feature of the case salient—namely, that the pre-manipulation person would not hurt a fly (as we say). I also issued that invitation to encourage readers to think of my fictional character as a real human being whose moral character resembles that of someone they know. This perspective is not easy to take when a story involves outlandish science fiction, but it is a useful perspective nonetheless. Finally, the bit about the person changing back to normal at the end of the day is primarily there for anyone tempted to think that the person is morally blameworthy partly because overt blame might improve her character.

Facts about Sally's history play an important role in the reason I offered for the judgments I make about her. So why do I settle for a negative historical constraint on free action and moral responsibility rather than claiming that any possible agent has to have been an agent for more than a few seconds in order to act freely and do things for which he is morally responsible and rather than claiming, in McKenna's words, that "What is required with respect to the causal springs of an agent's putatively free act is that she had a history in which she had the opportunity to fashion her evaluative standpoint for herself" (2012, p. 169)? The answer is simple. I provided it earlier in this chapter, in terms of Athena, a magical instant agent of mine. Because I have just been discussing minutelings, I frame it now in terms of an instant agent of this kind: I have not seen a convincing argument that would yield the judgments that my minuteling does not freely decide to shoot the prisoner and is not morally responsible for deciding to do that. For now, I am agnostic about the minuteling on these matters.

The minuteling is who he is for a minute. There is nothing more to him. But Sally's minute on the firing line is an aberration. There is a lot more to her than we see in that minute; most of the rest of it is very good; and we know that, if it were not for the manipulation, there would be no way on Earth that Sally would decide to shoot someone she believed to be innocent in order to find out what killing someone feels like. Such differences may help to account for some other differences: for example, someone's having a strong intuition that Sally is not morally responsible for deciding to shoot the prisoner while also having an intuition that the minuteling is morally responsible for his decision or while having no intuition about whether he is morally responsible for this.

McKenna 2012 ends with the following remark about certain "nonhistorical currents in our thinking about freedom and moral responsibility": They "seem to me to be by contrast with the historical conception more shallow; the notions of freedom and moral responsibility they commend turn out to be less important, less worth wanting. I am, however, at a loss to explain why exactly it is that I take this to be so" (p. 172). A view according to which my minuteling freely decides to shoot the prisoner and is morally responsible for deciding to do that may seem to some readers to be about as insubstantial as my minuteling is. But be this as it may, one can accept the "free" and "morally responsible" verdict about the minuteling's decision while consistently denying both that Sally freely decided to shoot the prisoner and that she was morally responsible for deciding to do that. And, of course, the grounds I have offered for these denials about Sally—grounds that cohere with the general idea behind my radical reversal suggestions—do not apply to the minuteling.[7]

McKenna discusses pros and cons, as he sees them, of historical and nonhistorical compatibilism. One advantage of the latter, he says, is that it does not have the "potential disadvantages of an historical thesis" (2012, p. 170). He adds: "But another, more compelling one is just that it gets its traction from a very basic moral insight—that once a person has come to be a . . . morally responsible agent, she ought to be evaluated for what she does and how she is, not how she came to be that way." Perhaps, with some qualifications, the alleged insight is true of relatively normal adult human beings in relatively normal circumstances. But when we turn our attention to the task of identifying conditions that are individually necessary and jointly sufficient for any possible agent's being morally responsible for an action, some strange and far-fetched thought experiments need to be considered. We then are in or near the realm of Suzie Instant, Athena, minutelings, and heavy-duty manipulation. As I see it, Chuck, in *One Good Day*, is not morally responsible for his good deeds even though unmanipulated Sally is morally responsible for hers. The pertinent difference between them is in how they came to be the way they were at the relevant times. Similarly, in my view, Sally is not morally responsible for her decision to shoot the prisoner even if Marty (or the minuteling) is morally responsible for his decision to do that. And again the pertinent difference between them is historical. If there is an element of truth in the alleged moral insight McKenna voiced, that element is consistent with the externalist compatibilist view I have floated, including its negative historical constraint.

3. INTERLUDE ON "COULD (NOT) HAVE DONE OTHERWISE" AND UNSHEDDABLE VALUES

I mentioned that my exchanges with Michael McKenna on the topic of manipulation have not quite clicked. I am partly responsible for that. Recall clause 2 of *NFM* (Section 1): "owing directly to those values, he could not have done otherwise than *A* in the circumstances (on a compatibilist reading of 'could have done otherwise')." The parenthetical clause is potentially misleading. What I meant to communicate in that clause is that incompatibilist standards for "could have done otherwise" are not in play, but I can see how someone might take me to mean that any (familiar) compatibilist reading of "could have done otherwise" is in play. When read the latter way, the clause definitely invites confusion. Not being able to "have done otherwise than *A* in the circumstances," as I understood that condition in my discussion of it in Mele 2006 (chap. 7), is, in fact, compatible with being able to do otherwise than *A* on a common compatibilist construal of that ability. An explanation of this puzzling-sounding remark is forthcoming.

One kind of case I had in mind there (see Mele 2006, pp. 167–74) was thrust into the philosophical limelight by Daniel Dennett. He contends that in cases like that of Martin Luther's registering his protest, "when I say that I cannot do otherwise I mean I cannot because I see so clearly what the situation is and because my rational control faculty is *not* impaired" (1984, p. 133). In this connection, Dennett reports a belief he has about himself: "it would be impossible to induce me to torture an innocent person by offering me a thousand dollars." In reply to an anticipated objection that he would torture an innocent person to save the whole world, Dennett writes, "That is a vastly different case. If what one is interested in is whether *under the specified circumstances* I could have done otherwise, then the other case mentioned is utterly irrelevant. I claimed it would not be possible to induce me to torture someone *for a thousand dollars* . . . . I claim that I could not do otherwise in any roughly similar case" (p. 133). I was especially interested, of course, in cases in which one deserves moral credit or blame for being such that one could not do otherwise than *A*, in roughly the sense of "could not do otherwise" at work in these passages from Dennett. For readers who would say that Chuck's "rational control faculty" or perception of the circumstances in *Thoroughly Bad Chuck is* impaired owing to his insensitivity to moral reasons for action, I add that I do not treat absence of impairment of this kind as a necessary condition for the (alleged) sort of inability at issue.[8]

It is open to a compatibilist to claim that what Dennett is describing is not literally being unable to do something ("in the circumstances," as both Dennett and I put it) but, instead, a weaker condition—for example, being very strongly disposed not to do it (in the circumstances). Once that claim is made, the question exactly what it is to be able to do something moves to center stage. This is an interesting question, to be sure. But it does not need to be answered to make significant progress on the dispute between internalists and externalists about moral responsibility (or free or autonomous action). I have chosen to bypass this difficult question here (but see Mele 2003b or 2017, chap. 4, for discussion).

Although I am bypassing the question just raised about the ability to do otherwise, a further comment on this ability is in order. It may be claimed that Luther was able to do otherwise than protest because, if he had taken himself to have a decisive reason to refrain, he would have refrained—and rationally so—on the basis of that reason. For example, he would have refrained if he had believed that, in the nick of time, God informed him that protesting would be wrong. It may be replied that not being able to do otherwise *in the circumstances*—which included Luther's having, in his opinion, a decisive reason to protest (and, of course, no discouraging news from

God)—is compatible with being able to do otherwise in the sense at issue. But, for reasons that will emerge shortly, this is an issue that can be skirted for my purposes.

Attention to a Luther-style story of mine presented in Mele 2006 along with a counterpart story involving manipulation will prove useful (see Mele 2006, pp. 167–70; also see Mele 1995, pp. 153–55). Imagine that Pat started his career as a father as a mediocre one. His own father had been very good to him, and Pat occasionally felt guilty about how little he did with and for his two children. After a couple of years as a mediocre parent, Pat freely embarked on a program of self-improvement. Part of his strategy was to spend more time with his kids, to make that more pleasant for himself by identifying and arranging activities that would be mutually enjoyable, and to focus his thinking about his kids, as much as possible, on their good properties and their welfare. For many parents, this sort of thing comes naturally, but for Pat it did not. To make a long story short, over the years, owing significantly to his self-improvement strategy, Pat became a wonderful father whose parental values were such that he could not do otherwise—in the Luther-style sense of that expression in play now—than make certain sacrifices for his children. Just today, he made such a sacrifice. He took out a huge loan to finance his daughter's first year at an exclusive liberal arts college. Pat's admirable unsheddable parental values were at work.

Compare Pat with Paul, another father of an eighteen-year-old daughter. Paul is a selfish man who has for many years reflectively and wholeheartedly identified with his selfish values. At least, that was true of him when he fell asleep last night. As he slept, Paul underwent some new-wave brainwashing. Paul's wealthy mother, without his knowledge, had hired a team of psychologists to determine what makes Pat tick and a team of brainwashers to make Paul like Pat (for just one day, if you like). The psychologists decided that Pat's hierarchy of values accounts for his wonderful parental behavior, and the brainwashers instilled the same hierarchy in Paul while eradicating all competing values. Paul is now, like Pat, an extremely caring parent with some unsheddable parental values. Largely as a result of Paul's new hierarchy of values, whatever upshot Pat's critical reflection about his own values and priorities would have, the same is true of critical reflection by Paul. His critical reflection would fully support his new values.

When Paul awakes, he recalls his daughter's wish to attend an exclusive liberal arts college, and he experiences a powerful desire to make that possible for her by taking out a huge loan. Naturally, Paul is amazed by this change in himself. He wonders what accounts for his remarkable concern for his daughter's welfare and why he now cares so little about buying himself a new car. Paul's hypothesis is that he simply has grown tired of his selfish ways, that he finally has come to understand the importance of father-daughter relationships, and that his powerful concern for his daughter's welfare had strangely been hidden from him. When he carefully reflects on his values, Paul finds that they fully support a life dedicated in significant part to his daughter's welfare, and he wholeheartedly embraces the idea of living such a life and the values that support it. When he thinks about his daughter's desire to attend the liberal arts college, it is obvious to him that he should take out the loan and that he very much wants to do so. Paul borrows the money later that day. Given his new parental values, he could not have done otherwise (in the Luther-style sense).

Paul's own considered values were erased and replaced in the brainwashing process, and some of his new values are unsheddable. He did not consent to the process. Nor was he even aware of it; he had no opportunity to resist. By instilling new values in Paul and eliminating old ones, the brainwashers gave his life a new direction that clashes with the considered principles and values he had before he was manipulated. He seems heteronomous to a significant extent, and he seems to be undeserving of moral credit for taking out the loan and to lack moral responsibility for that deed. This is how things seem to me, at least. Like Pat, Paul could not have done otherwise than borrow the money for his daughter's education (in the Luther-style sense); but whereas the history that accounts for this fact about Pat is compatible with his deserving moral credit for doing this and with his doing it freely, the process that accounts for the same fact about Paul seems not to be.

Now, either my Luther-style use of "could not have done otherwise" in my stories about Pat and Paul is acceptable or it is not. Either way, readers who agree with me about Pat and Paul will hold that Pat deserves moral credit for taking out the loan for his daughter and that Paul does not deserve moral credit for his parallel deed. It is unlikely that readers' intuitions and judgments about moral responsibility for the featured deeds in these stories will turn on whether their standards for its being the case that an agent could not have done otherwise in the circumstances are too exclusive to permit acceptance of my Luther-style use of the expression. The internal condition of these agents at the time—which includes unsheddable values (in my sense), of course—is what it is whether or not one is willing to count the Luther-style use of "could not have done otherwise" as a legitimate or useful use of that expression.[9]

A clause in *NFM* prompted the discussion in this section. For my purposes in this book, *NFM* may be replaced with the following statement, which is noncommittal on the ability to do otherwise and makes no reference to unsheddable values (nor is it restricted to overt actions):

> *NFMR*. An agent does not freely *A* and is not morally responsible for *A*-ing if the following is true: (1) for years and until manipulators got their hands on him, his system of values was such as to preclude his acquiring even a desire to perform an action of type *A*, much less an intention to perform an action of that

> type; (2) he was morally responsible for having a long-standing system of values with that property; (3) by means of very recent manipulation to which he did not consent and for which he is not morally responsible, his system of values was suddenly and radically transformed in such a way as to render *A*-ing attractive to him during *t*; and (4) the transformation ensures either (*a*) that although he is able during *t* intentionally to do otherwise than *A* during *t*, the only values that contribute to that ability are products of the very recent manipulation and are radically unlike any of his erased values (in content or in strength) or (*b*) that, owing to his new values, he has at least a Luther-style inability during *t* intentionally to do otherwise than *A* during *t*.

If a Luther-style inability is not a genuine inability, then 4*a* and 4*b* are not mutually exclusive. The featured deeds in such stories as *One Good Day, One Bad Day,* and *Bad Day Modified* satisfy the four conditions of *NFMR*. The same is true of my story about Paul in this section.

One last point completes this section. My notion of unsheddable values has been the subject of some confusion, as I have explained (Section 2). I accept some responsibility for that, as I did in this section for a potentially misleading clause that employed the expression "could have done otherwise." I have never offered a precise account of unsheddability; so the door is open for interpretations of it that do not fit what I had in mind. Because the conception of unsheddable values in McKenna 2012 is remote from mine, one can come closer to what I had in mind while still departing significantly from my intent. Here is an example. Suppose that it suddenly strikes a normally well-behaved young man as a good idea—a good thing—to join a crowd in hurling insults at some peaceful protestors and he suddenly desires to do so. He has a fleeting belief that his insulting the protestor would be a good thing along with a desire to do so, and he therefore values doing so, in my thin sense of "values." Suppose also that there is nothing the young man can do in the next few seconds to eradicate the belief nor to weaken the desire significantly and, within a few seconds, he hurls an insult. As I understand unsheddable values, the value at issue is not an unsheddable one even though the young man was not able at the time to shed it right then—before he acted on the desire. It does not run nearly deep enough for that. Someone else, moved perhaps by considerations of simplicity of expression, may be attracted to the idea that any value that one did not have time to shed before one acted on it should count as an unsheddable value.[10] Rather than pursue such issues about unsheddability, I leave the notion behind and forge ahead without it. *NFMR* is a step in that direction.

As I mentioned in Section 1, I developed my notion of unsheddable values in Mele 1995 to deal with the fact that to the extent to which a manipulated person can successfully counteract the effects of the manipulation, having been a victim of implanted values does not necessarily render him nonautonomous regarding the continued possession of those values. Implanted values that the manipulated person can easily eradicate or easily significantly attenuate do not pose a problem for autonomy in the sphere at issue—the sphere of continued value possession. Implanted values that are very highly resistant to such change are highly problematic for such autonomy. Now, continued possession of values is one thing and acting on the basis of values is another. Whereas in Mele 1995, as I explained in Section 1, my primary concern with manipulation was its bearing on a person's inner life, here, partly in response to McKenna, I have moved on to overt action. And when overt action is front and center, an action-featuring condition like *NFMR* 4 is a more appropriate and effective device than my notion of unsheddable values.

4. VARGAS ON INTERNALISM AND EXTERNALISM

In an article on moral responsibility and agents' histories, Manuel Vargas highlights "the basic agential structure of responsibility (BASR)" (2006, p. 363), which he describes as "a thin account of responsible agency" (p. 368). BASR includes "at least minimal rationality, sensitivity to justified moral norms, responsiveness to moral reasons, and the presence and normal operation of basic psychological features, including beliefs, pro-attitudes, and intentions" (p. 363). Vargas contends that "if BASR is present in a Brave New World [covert manipulation] case, the agent ought to be counted as a responsible agent because she has the capacities we are justified in fostering through moral influence" (pp. 366–67).

Nothing in Vargas's position in this article (2006) commits him to disagreeing with my asymmetrical moral responsibility judgments about Chuck in *Thoroughly Bad Chuck* and Sally in *One Bad Day*. To be sure, the agents in those stories are not, for example, responsive to moral reasons. But, obviously, holding that exhibiting BASR in an action is a *sufficient* condition for being morally responsible for that action does not commit one to holding that it is also a *necessary* condition for this; and Vargas maintains that some agents who lack BASR at the time of an action are nevertheless morally responsible for the action (see 2006, pp. 356–57, on drunk drivers). Because Chuck lacks "sensitivity to justified moral norms" and "responsiveness to moral reasons" when he kills one of his victims in *Thoroughly Bad Chuck*, he lacks BASR at the time. But it is open to Vargas to take a history-sensitive stand on Chuck, as he does on drunk drivers. (Chuck had BASR when he embarked on his heart-hardening project.) And it is open to him to judge that Chuck is morally responsible for killing someone while also judging that Sally—who lacks BASR when she kills George—is *not* morally responsible for killing George in *One Bad Day*.

Vargas's position and mine come into conflict over some other pairs of stories. In *One Good Day,* Chuck has BASR on the day at issue. So, given the claim about Brave New World cases that I quoted earlier, Vargas presumably would count Chuck as morally responsible for his charitable deeds in *One Good Day.*[11] I, on the other hand, have contended that Chuck is not morally responsible for those deeds.

An interesting feature of Vargas's "revisionist" view of moral responsibility is that it allows us to "be open to the idea that ordinary thinking about responsibility may well be historical in the way historicists insist, while maintaining that an adequate theory will depart from the folk concept in counterintuitive ways" (2006, p. 372). So Vargas can claim that even if the overwhelming majority of people have a very strong intuitive reaction to *One Good Day,* and even if that reaction is that Chuck deserves no moral credit for his good deeds on the day at issue and therefore is not morally responsible for those good deeds, he is, in fact, morally responsible for them.

How does Vargas get to this point? He contends that "the difficulty with trying to shoehorn our best philosophical theories into the constraints of our presumably contingent and culturally inherited intuitions is well-illustrated by the intuition stand-off that characterizes the history/structure debate" (2006, p. 371). Earlier, he mentions what he describes as the "apparent intractability of the issue" (p. 352; also see p. 362); and, borrowing an expression from John Fischer, he represents the situation as an apparent "dialectical stalemate" (p. 359). Vargas contends that "moderate revisionism gives us a way out by abandoning the project of comprehensive intuition vindication" (p. 362). The focus, instead, is on "providing a normatively adequate foundation for our responsibility-characteristic practices, attitudes and beliefs." This is where BASR enters the scene.

I will comment on both of the themes just sketched—the "intractability" or "stalemate" theme and the theme of providing a "normatively adequate foundation." I start with the former.[12] When have we reached the point of an "intuition stand-off"? If, say, one philosopher—perhaps a very accomplished one—asserts in print that he or she lacks the intuition that Chuck is not morally responsible for his good deeds in *One Good Day* and ten philosophers assert in print that they do have this intuition, do we then have an "intuition stand-off"? If so, at least some intuition stand-offs are not, in principle, cause for much worry. For all we know, the lone philosopher's lacking the intuition at issue about Chuck is explained by his or her being in the grip of an unacceptable theory. This philosopher might even be self-deceived in believing that he or she lacks the intuition. Generating related hypotheses is left as an exercise for the reader.

Suppose now that some other philosophers attempt to assist the lone philosopher by arguing for the thesis that the intuition that Chuck is not morally responsible for his good deeds in *One Good Day* is not clearly warranted. If there was an intuition stand-off already, has it become more serious? Or if there was not yet such a stand-off, has one now been reached? Not necessarily. The *quality* of the new arguments is directly relevant. For example, the arguments might all feature an undefended premise about a connection between instant agents and Chuck (see Section 2), and they might all be far from persuasive.

This is not to say that there never are any genuine, serious clashes of intuitions. When the issues are important and such a clash exists, I agree with Vargas that it would be nice to find a way to keep the debate alive and to make it productive.

I turn to the second theme. If it is true that the overwhelming majority of people have a strong intuition that Chuck is not morally responsible for his good deeds in *One Good Day,* how could endorsing the claim that he is not morally responsible for those deeds obstruct the project of "providing a normatively adequate foundation for our responsibility-characteristic practices, attitudes and beliefs" (Vargas 2006, p. 362)? One worry may be that the combination of this claim about Chuck and some collection of known truths would be obstructive. Of course, someone who thinks that there is a genuine worry of this kind should try to motivate it. As things stand, I see nothing obstructive about the claim at issue about Chuck. (I return to this claim shortly.)

Elsewhere, I have suggested that some compatibilists may worry that a philosopher who grants that agents' histories have a bearing of the sort I have been discussing on their moral responsibility for their actions must also grant that agents' having *deterministic* histories bears on this too, and in a way that undermines compatibilism (Mele 1995, p. 158; also see Fischer and Ravizza 1994, p. 444). I have argued that this worry is unfounded (Mele 1995, pp. 158, 173, 187–89; 2006, p. 166), I commented on it briefly in Chapter 2, Section 3, and I return to it in Chapter 4.

Vargas does not say in the article I have been discussing (Vargas 2006) whether he has or lacks the intuition that Chuck is not morally responsible for his good deeds in *One Good Day*. As far as I can see, if he has it, he can modify his "semistructuralist" position to accommodate an endorsement of the claim that Chuck is not morally responsible for these deeds without obstructing his foundational project. If he lacks this intuition, an argument that the intuition is misleading might prove interesting. Of course, it is fair to ask me why I believe that the intuition that Chuck is not morally responsible for his good deeds is not misleading. My radical reversal suggestion about *One Good Day* is relevant here, and I return to it shortly.

Recall Vargas's assertion that "if BASR is present in a Brave New World case, the agent ought to be counted as a responsible agent because she has the capacities we are justified in fostering through moral influence" (2006, pp. 366–67). Consider the following conditional internalist proposition:

> *P*. For any conceptually possible agent *S* and any conceptually possible action *A*, if *S* had the wholly nonhistorical "capacities we are justified in fostering through moral influence" when *S A*-ed and those capacities were suitably at work in producing *A*, *S* is morally responsible for *A*.

A comment on the expression "wholly nonhistorical capacities" is in order before *P* is examined. Someone might suggest that the following capacity is one that we are justified in fostering through moral influence: a capacity to express in action values that one is morally responsible for possessing owing partly to past actions for which one was morally responsible. But it has a historical dimension; it is not a wholly nonhistorical capacity and therefore is not a capacity of the sort to which *P* applies.

Is *P* true? One proposal is that *P* is falsified by *One Good Day*—that the story is a successful counterexample to *P*. Imagine that millions of sane people and thousands of sane philosophers are presented with this story and over 99% of each group agree that *P*'s antecedent is satisfied and sincerely assert that, even so, they have a strong intuition that Chuck is not morally responsible for his good deeds. Imagine also that Vargas himself has the intuition that Chuck is not morally responsible for his good deeds in *One Good Day*. Even then, given that Vargas's "moderate revisionism... abandon[s] the project of comprehensive intuition vindication" (2006, p. 362), it is open to him to contend that, in fact, Chuck is morally responsible for his good deeds in *One Good Day* and that *P* is true. Some readers may find this disturbing. In any case, if an argument were advanced for *P*'s truth, it could be assessed in typical ways. In the absence of such an argument, the imagined facts should be taken to constitute significant grounds for skepticism about *P*.

It merits mention that a revisionist does not need to set intuitions aside entirely. A philosopher can abandon the project of *comprehensive* intuition vindication while seeking to accommodate very widely shared strong intuitions.[13] Should it turn out that the intuition that Chuck is not morally responsible for his good deeds in *One Good Day* is of this kind, Vargas might deem it reasonable to modify his position on moral responsibility accordingly.

I certainly am not suggesting that intuitions are the final word on philosophical matters. Sometimes we find that our intuitions clash with the intuitions of others. When that happens, there often is room for discussion and progress, as I explained in Chapter 2. If we were to set intuitions aside entirely, we would be significantly reducing our resources for assessing proposals like *P*.

I have highlighted internalist proposition *P* for a reason. In the absence of a powerful argument for *P*, one who is attracted to an account of moral responsibility that, like Vargas's, features attention to "capacities we are justified in fostering through moral influence" (2006, pp. 366–67) may reasonably seek to accommodate in such an account the judgment that Chuck is not morally responsible for his good deeds in *One Good Day*.[14]

In his recent book, Vargas responds to my radical reversal suggestion about Chuck in *One Good Day*. He reports that he is "unpersuaded that *One Good Day* works against" his account of moral responsibility and offers several reasons for this (2013, p. 300). The first is that stories of this kind "invite questions about personal identity." He contends that "there is ample room for skepticism about whether identity holds up across such transformations." The second is that "*One Good Day* is a case about praise and this raises some puzzles of its own when used as a probe." Vargas writes, "Although I won't try to make the argument here, I think we're pretty bad about knowing when and how to praise." (I will follow suit and not offer a counterargument.) He also reports his inclination to think that Chuck "really is praiseworthy" for his good deeds, given that he "really is recognizing moral considerations and self-governing in light of them." Finally, Vargas offers a "diagnosis of our reticence to view Chuck as praiseworthy. It derives from the fact of his having done those terrible things in the past, and his not feeling guilty (even now), coupled by his continuing failure to make right for his wrongs."

I start with personal identity. Consider the claim that the person who wakes up in Chuck's bed in *One Good Day* is not Chuck. How would we make sense of this? The most straightforward way is to say that Chuck died or otherwise went out of existence during the night and another person who looks exactly like Chuck and has pseudo-memories that strongly resemble Chuck's actual memories came into existence. And what should we say when, at the end of the day, the manipulation is undone? If the radical change in Chuck's values was enough to kill him or otherwise ensure that he went out of existence that night, then one would suppose that the radical change in the new person's values would have the same effect on him. And what about the man who wakes up in Chuck's bed the day after *One Good Day*? Did Chuck come back to life? Or do we now have a third person who looks just like the first two and has pseudo-memories that strongly resemble their actual memories. If the former, we have what sounds like a miracle. And if the latter, we have, in addition to dead Chuck, two instant agents, one of whom existed for a day. Another route one may consider traveling attributes to Chuck a gappy existence that excludes the period occupied by *One Good Day* and posits the existence of a different person who replaces Chuck during that period. Readers are free to choose a path. The path I choose is the easiest one to travel; it is to say that Chuck—that person—persists through the value changes. Persons are one kind of thing, and moral personalities, moral characters, and practical identities are another (or others).[15]

Vargas's "diagnosis of our reticence to view Chuck as praiseworthy" is creative but unpersuasive. Imagine another version of *One Good Day* in which Chuck had been especially nasty to homeless families and Girl Scouts, and it is partly for that reason that the manipulators chose to implant Sally's values in him rather than the values of another moral saint with very different admirable projects. As a consequence of the manipulation, Chuck feels guilty about his evil behavior, and he views the day's activities as a way of beginning "to make right for his wrongs." I am no less inclined to see Chuck as lacking moral responsibility for his good deeds in this case—and for the same reasons offered in my radical reversal suggestion about the earlier version of *One Good Day*. Readers are free to consult their own intuitions about the two versions of *One Good Day* at issue now and to see whether the modification has a significant effect on them.

That leaves Vargas's reported inclination to think that Chuck is praiseworthy for his good deeds in *One Good Day*. If the inclination rests on the belief that Chuck is replaced by someone else in that story, then, in my view, it rests on a false belief. (I should add that, if the belief were true, the person who wakes up in Chuck's bed in *One Good Day* would be an instant agent.) If Vargas's inclination is about the person I view as Chuck—a person who persists over the days at issue—then perhaps he and I have significantly different conceptions of what it is to be worthy or deserving of praise (or positive moral credit) for an action. In this connection, a rough analogy from a non-moral realm may be interesting. A novice at chess who plays very poorly receives a chip implant that gives him amazing chess skills for an hour. He defeats a grand master in a brilliantly played game. Does this man deserve praise for playing a brilliant game or for defeating his opponent? I say no. If you, dear reader, sincerely say yes, I suspect that we mean different things by "deserves praise." To be sure, chess enthusiasts who witnessed the game and presumed normal conditions would be bowled over by the man's performance and heap praise on him. Would they do the same if they knew the whole story? As I see things, if there is deserved praise in this story, it all goes to the designers of the chip. (On nonspecialists' reactions to a pair of stories of this kind about a novice chess player, see the Appendix.)

Here is another non-moral case of enhancement. It has a greater impact on some people. Alfred, an elderly man who was a weight-lifter in his youth, has a dream in which he wins a certain weight-lifting competition. Impressed by the unusual vividness of the dream, he enters the competition. Eleven enormous, powerful men do their best, and then it is Alfred's turn. In the dream, he performs a clean and jerk of 1500 pounds, beating the second-place competitor by 1000 pounds. So that is what he attempts. To everyone's utter amazement, Alfred succeeds; and he exerts no more effort than he normally would to clean and jerk twenty pounds. The aliens who caused him to have the vivid dream also gave him super strength for a short time. I do not see how Alfred can deserve praise for lifting the weight.[16] (See the Appendix for nonspecialists' reactions to a story of this kind.)

I am not suggesting that Vargas's general approach to understanding moral responsibility should be rejected. My claim is much more modest: A philosopher who takes that approach would do well to accommodate the judgment that Chuck is not morally responsible for his good deeds in *One Good Day*.

5. MORE ON RADICAL REVERSALS

I have had a lot to say about radical reversal cases, both in the present chapter and in Chapter 2. In my view, no successful analysis of moral responsibility for actions will ignore such cases. I close this chapter with a brief illustration of how ignoring them can lead one astray.

Chandra Sripada reports on experimental philosophy studies he conducted of lay responses to some cases of manipulation (2012). No radical reversal stories were considered. He closes the article as follows:

> Results showed that subjects' tendency to judge that a manipulated agent is unfree was fully explained by their judgments that the manipulated agent suffers from damage to certain key psychological capacities. These results strongly support the view that intuitions in manipulation cases are responsive to impairments in just the kinds of psychological capacities that compatibilists have long claimed are the basis for free will. They also put serious pressure on incompatibilists' use of manipulation cases to support their position. (p. 588)

Sripada mentions in a note that some compatibilists "build extra historical conditions on top of" internal requirements, citing Fischer and Ravizza 1998 and Mele 2006; and he adds that "the results of the studies reported in this paper suggest that these extra historical conditions are actually *unnecessary*" (p. 567 n. 2).

My own defense of a negative historical requirement for moral responsibility for actions (and for acting autonomously or freely) has always featured radical reversal cases (Mele 1995, 2006), as does the defense offered in this book. In these cases, one of the two kinds of impairment Sripada mentions is definitely absent, assuming that the impairment is a purely internal matter. This is "deep self discordance" (2012, p. 570): the "surface layer . . . of the superficial values, attitudes, and behavioral tendencies instilled by manipulation" are discordant with a "deeper layer" of persisting "values, attitude[s], and core commitments" (p. 571). In my radical reversal stories, there is no such discordance. New values are not implanted on top of older discordant ones that persist. Any prior values that would have conflicted with the implanted ones were erased. I suppose someone might claim that, for example, Chuck in *One Good Day* does not freely help the Girl Scouts because the values that motivate his behavior are discordant with values that he *used to* have. But, of course, that claim appeals to a fact about Chuck's *history*. It is not an internalist claim.

The other kind of impairment Sripada mentions is informational (see Mele 1995, pp. 179–82): specifically, "significant corrupting of information used by the [agent] as a basis to make decisions" (2012, p. 569). As far as I can see, there is no such impairment in *One Good Day*. One may claim that this kind of impairment is present in *One Bad Day* (and the spin-off stories about Sally), because Sally's new values include false beliefs about what is good. But notice that she has the same values as unmanipulated Chuck; and, if I am right, Chuck is morally responsible for his bad deeds and performs them freely. If the impairment at issue helps get Sally off the hook for killing George but does not help get Chuck off the hook for killing Don, why is that? I have offered an answer, which includes my radical reversal suggestion about Sally; and Sripada provides no answer to this question. It may be claimed that Sally is morally responsible for killing George and does so freely. But Sripada's studies do not support that claim. The studies tell us nothing about lay responses to radical reversal stories.

Sripada contends that his results support the following conclusion: "our intuitions in manipulation cases track the features that compatibilists say they track (i.e., the agent's possessing impaired psychological capacities) and do not track the features that incompatibilists say they track (i.e., the agent's lack of ultimate control over his or her actions)" (2012, pp. 582–83).[17] This is the source of the alleged "serious pressure on incompatibilists' use of manipulation cases to support their position" in a passage I quoted from Sripada 2012. My own intuitions about such cases as *One Good Day* and *One Bad Day* do not track impaired psychological capacities—even when I am wearing my compatibilist hat. Chuck's relevant psychological capacities in *One Good Day* are no more impaired than unmanipulated Sally's are; and, even so, I have asymmetrical intuitions about these agents. My intuitions are tracking something else, something captured in part by my radical reversal suggestions. And, once again, the alleged informational impairment itself cannot be what gets Sally off the hook in *One Bad Day* (and the spin-off stories), if Chuck is not off the hook for killing Don, despite being equally informationally impaired. My asymmetrical intuitions about manipulated Sally and unmanipulated Chuck respect this point and are tracking something that includes facts about Chuck's and Sally's histories. (A study I conducted of radical reversal stories is discussed in the Appendix. Readers will see that the majority of respondents make externalist judgments about moral responsibility in the good-to-bad and bad-to-good stories they read.)

In this chapter I have highlighted the importance of radical reversal stories, exposed some misunderstandings of my externalist view about moral responsibility for actions, and defended that view against some alleged threats. In the following chapter I take up an alleged threat of another kind to my externalist view.[18]

Chapter 4

Must Compatibilists Be Internalists?

The purpose of this chapter is to identify and assess some lines of thought that may lie behind the pull some compatibilists feel toward internalism. These lines of thought build bridges from compatibilism to internalism. I argue that they are seriously defective.

1. WHAT MIGHT INTERNALIST COMPATIBILISTS BE THINKING?

One line of thought of the sort I intend to examine shows up in the following passage from Harry Frankfurt. I briefly discussed an excerpt from it in Chapter 2:

> A manipulator may succeed, through his interventions, in providing a person not merely with particular feelings and thoughts but with a new character. That person is then morally responsible for the choices and the conduct to which having this character leads. *We are inevitably fashioned and sustained, after all, by circumstances over which we have no control.* The causes to which we are subject may also change us radically,

> without thereby bringing it about that we are not morally responsible agents. It is irrelevant whether those causes are operating by virtue of the natural forces that shape our environment or whether they operate through the deliberately manipulative designs of other human agents. (Frankfurt 2002, p. 28; emphasis added)

Richard Double may be thinking along Frankfurt's lines when he contends, in a passage I quoted and briefly discussed in Chapter 2, that "the internalistic view is implicit in compatibilism" and "compatibilism has not a chance of plausibility without [internalism], since otherwise the incompatibilist abhorrence of determinism will destroy it" (1991, pp. 56–57).

In a similar vein, we have the following from Gary Watson:

> For the compatibilist, the constitutive conditions of free agency do not conceptually depend on their origins. In this sense, free and responsible agency is not an historical notion. Consequently, compatibilism is committed to the conceptual possibility that free and responsible agents, and free and responsible exercises of their agency, are products of super-powerful designers. For consider any compatibilist account of the conditions of free agency, C. It is possible for C to obtain in a causally deterministic world. If that is possible, then it is possible that a super-powerful being intentionally creates a C-world, by bringing about the relevant antecedent conditions in accordance with the relevant laws. This possibility follows from the general point that the conditions of responsibility do not necessarily depend upon their causal origins. (1999, pp. 360–61)

Watson adds: "If we define a robot as a creature whose existence and detailed 'program' were brought about by design, then the foregoing reasoning commits compatibilists to the possibility that free agents are robots" (p. 361).

I return to the quoted passages later. They serve as background now. Another bit of background is the point that stories of some different kinds pose apparent threats of different kinds to internalist compatibilism. To illustrate this point, I rehearse a story spun in Mele 2006 and then call attention to some stories discussed in previous chapters.

Here is an *original-design* story from Mele 2006 (p. 188).

> *Ernie*. Diana creates a zygote *Z* in Mary. She combines *Z*'s atoms as she does because she wants a certain event *E* to occur thirty years later. From her knowledge of the state of the universe just prior to her creating *Z* and the laws of nature of her deterministic universe, she deduces that a zygote with precisely *Z*'s constitution located in Mary will develop into an ideally self-controlled agent who, in thirty years, will judge, on the basis of rational deliberation, that it is best to *A* and will *A* on the basis of that judgment, thereby bringing about *E* . . . . Thirty years later, Ernie is a mentally healthy, ideally self-controlled person who regularly exercises his powers of self-control and has no relevant compelled or coercively produced attitudes. Furthermore, his beliefs are conducive to informed deliberation about all matters that concern him, and he is a reliable deliberator.[1]

Diana assembles *Z* as she does in Mary so that *E* will happen. Of course, in doing this, thereby ensuring that Ernie will bring about *E* by *A*-ing thirty years later, Diana ensures much more. A complete description of the state of the universe just after Diana creates *Z*—including *Z*'s constitution—together with a complete statement of the laws of nature, entails a true statement of everything Ernie will ever do. In a version of this story, Diana does what she does in order to ensure everything that Ernie does (Mele 2006, pp. 189–90). Also, to block the claim that Ernie is not morally responsible for what he does only because another agent—Diana—is morally responsible for all of Ernie's actions, it may be supposed that Diana is not morally responsible for anything because she is stark raving mad and has no grasp of morality (Mele 2006, p. 198 n. 6). These additional details should be regarded as official parts of Ernie's story.

Consider the following argument (see Mele 2013b, p. 176; also see Mele 2006, p. 189).

1. Ernie is not morally responsible for anything he does.
2. Concerning moral responsibility of the beings into whom the zygotes develop, there is no significant difference between the way Ernie's zygote comes to exist and the way any normal human zygote comes to exist in a deterministic world.
3. So in no possible deterministic world in which a human being develops from a normal human zygote is that human being morally responsible for anything he or she does.

Because the conclusion is specifically about human beings who develop from a normal human zygote, it does not take us all the way to incompatibilism. But, of course, typical compatibilists reject this conclusion. I add that by "no significant difference" in 2, I mean no difference that would warrant asymmetrical moral-responsibility verdicts about actions. Readers will notice that the argument is enthymematic. Something needs to be added to secure validity, a matter that I take up in Chapter 5, Section 5. But the present version will do for present purposes.

We should not be surprised to find seasoned compatibilists rejecting premise 1. They might tell us that they knew all along, for reasons of the kind Watson describes, that they were committed to holding that an agent with Ernie's properties is morally responsible for his actions, and they might offer to explain why what they are committed to is true. In my own view (Mele 2006, pp. 192–93), this is the line compatibilists should take; a powerful argument for the falsity of premise 1 would be especially welcome.[2] Some philosophers have argued that premise 2 should be rejected (Barnes 2015; Deery and Nahmias 2017; Schlosser 2015; Waller 2014). I will not pursue that interesting idea here.[3]

Some other stories of mine feature manipulation-induced *radical reversals* in agents' hard-won values. Recall, for example, *One Bad Day* and *One Good Day*. Important differences between Ernie's story and these radical reversal stories will emerge.

Return to Double's claims that "the internalistic view is implicit in compatibilism" and that "compatibilism has not a chance of plausibility without [internalism], since otherwise the incompatibilist abhorrence of determinism will destroy it" (1991, pp. 56–57). I already have offered a partial response to these claims (Chapter 2, Section 3). Here I go further.

As I mentioned, the alleged problem that Double has in mind is that once agents' histories are allowed to have a relevance of the sort I claim to find in, for example, *One Bad Day*, their having *deterministic* histories is relevant as well, and in a way that undermines compatibilism. This formulation of the alleged problem is vague. But, as I observed elsewhere (Mele 1995, p. 158, 2013b, p. 171), there are ways of making the worry more precise. For example, it may be thought that if the brainwashing involved in *One Bad Day* gets Sally off the hook for killing George, it does so only if it *deterministically causes* crucial psychological events or states and that determinism consequently is in danger of being identified as the real culprit.

This more precise worry is misguided. Suppose that *Thoroughly Bad Chuck* and *One Bad Day* are set in a deterministic world. And consider the assertion that if Sally is off the hook, what gets her off the hook is the fact that the brainwashing deterministically caused various effects. To test the claim, I introduce indeterminism into *One Bad Day*. (The first version of this story presented in this book is silent on whether the setting is deterministic or indeterministic.) In the new version of the story, there was a tiny chance that the brainwashing would produce new values that fell short of the full strength of Chuck's values, and there was a tiny chance that even if the brainwashing did not fall short in value production, Sally would not act on her new values. In both connections, the only open alternative was Sally's suffering a breakdown that would prevent her from acting. As it happens, full-strength Chuck-like values were indeterministically produced in Sally, and those values were involved in the indeterministic causation of Sally's intentionally killing George. I submit that the overwhelming majority of readers who judge that Sally is not responsible for the killing in the original case will make the same judgment in the modified case.[4] If these judgments are correct, it is false that the brainwashing's getting Sally off the hook depends on its deterministically causing crucial psychological states or events.

2. DIFFERENCES: ORIGINAL DESIGNS AND RADICAL REVERSALS

Recall premise 2 of the argument I formulated in connection with Ernie's story: Concerning moral responsibility of the beings into whom the zygotes develop, there is no significant difference between the way Ernie's zygote comes to exist and the way any normal human zygote comes to exist in a deterministic world. An analogous but more specific claim about Sally is the following: (*B2*) Concerning moral responsibility for the actions at issue, there is no significant difference between the way Sally comes to have the values on which she acts in *One Bad Day* and any of the ways in which unmanipulated human beings come to have such values in a deterministic world. As

I have indicated, by "no significant difference" I mean no difference that would warrant asymmetrical moral-responsibility verdicts about these actions.

As I observed in Mele 2006 (p. 190), a defense of premise 2 might begin with the question of how it can matter for the purposes of moral responsibility whether, in a deterministic world, a zygote with *Z*'s exact constitution was produced by a supremely intelligent agent with Diana's effective intentions or instead in the way zygotes are normally produced. Imagine a deterministic world *W** that is a lot like Ernie's world, *W*, but in which *Z* comes into being in Mary in the normal way and at the same time. It is conceivable that, in *W**, throughout his life, Mary's child, Bernie, does exactly what Ernie does in *W*, down to the smallest detail, expressing values and motives that mirror Ernie's (well, setting aside how they sign checks and the like; they have different names, after all). Suppose this is so. Then, one might contend that, given the additional facts that, in both worlds, the featured agent (Ernie in *W* and Bernie in *W**) has no say about what causes *Z*, no say about the rest of the universe at that time, and no say about what the laws of nature are, the cross-world difference in what caused *Z* does not support any cross-world difference in moral responsibility.

Turn now to *One Bad Day*, the explicitly indeterministic variant of that story sketched in Section 1, and *Bad Day Modified* (in which Sally becomes a value twin of a Chuck who had not quite completed his heart-hardening project). There are differences between how Sally acquired the values that her killing of George expressed and the way Chuck acquired his matching values, just as there are differences (of another kind) in how Ernie and Bernie acquired their values. Might compatibilists, consistently with their compatibilism, maintain that these differences between Sally and Chuck are morally significant and, more specifically, that, in light of them, although Chuck is morally responsible for his killing of Don, Sally is not morally responsible for her killing of George? It is true that both designed Ernie and undesigned Bernie have no say about the factors mentioned in the preceding paragraph. And Sally had no say about her coming to have the nasty values she acquires in *One Bad Day* and the variants of that story mentioned here. But on the values front, unmanipulated Chuck did have a say; he worked hard to increase his hard-heartedness, and he succeeded. Is it legitimate for a compatibilist to appeal to that difference between Chuck and Sally in defending the asymmetrical claims at issue about the killings?

In Chapter 2, I motivated what I dubbed a *radical reversal suggestion* about *Bad Day Modified*. My suggestion about Sally in that story is that her pre-transformation character was sufficiently good that killing George was *not even an option for her*; and the combination of this fact with the fact that Sally was morally responsible (to a significant extent) for that character, facts about her history that account for her moral responsibility for that character, facts about her post-manipulation values and associated abilities, and the facts that account for her killing George suffices for her not being morally responsible for killing him. As I observed in Chapter 3, the underlying idea applies as follows to Chuck in *One Good Day*. His pre-transformation character was sufficiently bad that kind deeds were *not even an option for him*; and the combination of this fact with the fact that Chuck was morally responsible (to a significant extent) for that character, facts about his history that account for his moral responsibility for that character, facts about his post-manipulation values and associated abilities, and the facts that account for his good deeds suffices for his not being morally responsible for those deeds. If he were morally responsible for them, he would deserve some credit for them from a moral point of view. But, as I see it, he deserves no moral credit at all for those deeds.

One point to be made now is that even if premise 2 in the argument about Ernie is true, and even if symmetrical judgments about whether Ernie and Bernie are morally responsible for their actions are correct, we should not infer from this that symmetrical judgments about whether Chuck and Sally are morally responsible for their killings—and for their good actions when unmanipulated Sally and *One Good Day* are at issue—are also correct. My original-design story is very different from my radical reversal stories—too different to move easily from symmetrical judgments in the former connection to the conclusion that symmetrical judgments also are correct in the latter connection. This is not to say that the move cannot be made. But making it convincingly would require a convincing argument.

3. ASSESSING AN INTERNALIST COMPATIBILIST LINE OF THOUGHT

It is time to return to the remarks by Watson and Frankfurt quoted at the beginning of Section 1 (conveniently placed so that readers can find them with little effort). I have already commented in this chapter on the remark by Double that is quoted there. My concern is a certain internalist compatibilist line of thought that applies to the stories discussed in this chapter.

The opening two sentences of the passage from Watson seem dismissive of history-sensitive compatibilism. Here they are again: "For the compatibilist, the constitutive conditions of free agency do not conceptually depend on their origins. In this sense, free and responsible agency is not an historical notion." Consider compatibilists who hold that Chuck—unlike Sally—does not freely help the Girl Scouts and is not morally responsible for helping them, owing to how he acquired the motives at work in his actions. Such compatibilists seemingly employ notions of free action and moral responsibility with an externalist component. An argument that compatibilism—or any compatibilist view worth taking seriously—commits them to rejecting this component might lead them to believe that they are confused. The pair of sentences I quoted obviously is not an argument for this. But there is more to the passage under consideration.

The third through sixth sentences of the quoted passage do the real work, and they highlight original design. Plainly, the design Watson contemplates is much more ambitious than the design at work in my story about Ernie. I have no quarrel with the main thrust of these sentences.

This brings us to the seventh and final sentence of the passage: "This possibility follows from the general point that the conditions of responsibility do not necessarily depend upon their causal origins."[5] The possibility at issue is that "a super-powerful being intentionally creates a C-world"—that is, a world in which proposed compatibilist sufficient conditions for free agency are satisfied—"by bringing about the relevant antecedent conditions in accordance with the relevant laws." Even if this possibility follows from the alleged "general point"—that is, from an internalist thesis (see note 5)—one may consistently accept the possibility and reject the general point. That the only human being in my office now is an adult male follows from the general claim that all human beings are adult males. Even so, and without contradiction, I accept the claim about the human being in this office and reject the general claim. Similarly, a compatibilist apparently may consistently accept the possibility Watson identifies while rejecting the alleged "general point"—that is, the internalist thesis he is advocating. For example, for all that Watson has *argued* here, a compatibilist may—without contradiction—reject various conditional internalist views on grounds having to do with radical reversal cases while agreeing with Watson about some cases of original design.

Assume that unmanipulated Sally is morally responsible for some of her kind actions even if her world is deterministic. With this assumption in place, if my radical reversal suggestion about *One Good*

Day is true, there are pairs of cases in which agents satisfy the same alleged internalist compatibilist sufficient conditions for moral responsibility for an action and, even so, asymmetrical moral responsibility judgments are correct. What makes the difference is a difference in history.

Here is a proposed history-involving claim about an agent's being morally responsible for *A*-ing:

> *RR*. Take an agent who, owing significantly to a lengthy series of actions he performed, was morally responsible for being thoroughly vicious and for being such that performing kind actions was not even an option for him. If, without his consent, his nasty values were erased and replaced overnight with the values of a moral saint in a way that bypassed his capacities for control over his mental life and he retains no preexisting value that is expressed in his performing a kind action, *A*, that he performs immediately after the value-engineering procedure, an action that expresses new, implanted values, he is not morally responsible for *A*-ing.[6]

Nothing in the line of reasoning in the passage from Watson justifies rejecting this history-sensitive claim. The reasoning in that passage is about original design and its bearing on compatibilism. Radical reversal cases are a distinct matter. The third sentence of the passage asserts that a commitment to "the conceptual possibility that free and responsible agents, and free and responsible exercises of their agency, are products of super-powerful designers" is a *consequence* of a compatibilist assertion (*NH*) that "free and responsible agency is not an historical notion." But no argument is offered for the claim that compatibilism (or any compatibilist view worth taking seriously) includes a commitment to *NH*—a commitment to an assertion that *does* contradict *RR*. *NH* is a statement of internalism (about "free and responsible agency"), and true symmetrical judgments about agents who are products of original design and undesigned counterparts do not themselves get us all the way to *NH*.[7]

The passage I quoted from Frankfurt at the beginning of Section 1 tackles character implantation head on. I reproduce the sentence from it that I italicized there: (*SI*) "We are inevitably fashioned and sustained, after all, by circumstances over which we have no control."[8] *SI* is supposed to help us see why, when a manipulator installs "a new character" in a person, "that person is then morally responsible for the choices and the conduct to which having that character leads" (provided, presumably, that having that character does not preclude the person's meeting conditions Frankfurt deems necessary for moral responsibility). But, as I observed in Chapter 2, *SI* does not entail that we "have no control" at all regarding any of our "circumstances" (again, Frankfurt says "by," not "by and only by"). For example, it does not entail that no recovering alcoholic has any control at all over whether, in a few minutes, his circumstances will include being within arm's reach of a glass of whiskey. And when we focus on control in the present context, it is salient that whereas Chuck in *One Good Day* exercised no control in the process that gave rise to his saintly, Sally-like system of values and identifications, Sally, by hypothesis, exercised significant control in fashioning her system of values and identifications. Frankfurt is committed to holding that that difference between Chuck and Sally is "irrelevant to the questions of whether [they perform their good deeds] freely or [are] morally responsible for performing them" (1988, p. 54); and, to echo a point I made in Chapter 2, he may contend that even if many people do have some control over some of their "circumstances," Sally is simply morally responsible for an extra item that Chuck is not—having saintly values. The contention is that both people are morally responsible for their kind deeds, and that Sally, but not Chuck, is morally responsible for having become a moral saint.

Return to premise 2 of the argument about Ernie's story: Concerning moral responsibility of the beings into whom the zygotes develop, there is no significant difference between the way Ernie's zygote comes to exist and the way any normal human zygote comes to exist in a deterministic world. An analogous claim about Chuck that emphatically takes into account the idea that Sally may be morally responsible for something in addition to her good deeds is the following: (*C2*) Concerning their moral responsibility specifically for their good deeds and nothing else, there is no significant difference between the way Chuck comes to have the values on which he acts in *One Good Day* and any of the ways in which unmanipulated human beings come to have such values in a deterministic world. Obviously, my radical reversal suggestion about *One Good Day* is at odds with *C2*. Does the line of reasoning in the passage under consideration from Frankfurt 2002 show that *C2* is on firmer ground than this suggestion?

The remainder of the passage reads as follows:

> [*F1*] The causes to which we are subject may also change us radically, without thereby bringing it about that we are not morally responsible agents. [*F2*] It is irrelevant whether those causes are operating by virtue of the natural forces that shape our environment or whether they operate through the deliberately manipulative designs of other human agents.

I have labeled the sentences here for ease of reference.

F1 mentions radical change. A sudden change from atheism to theism or vice versa seems radical; and I agree that such a change may be caused without the causes bringing it about that the person who underwent the change is not a morally responsible agent. But this point is utterly consistent with the truth of my radical reversal suggestions. What would undermine those suggestions is a convincing argument that changes of the kind featured in my radical reversal stories may be caused in the way they are caused in those stories without it being the case that, as a consequence, the agent is not morally responsible for the featured deeds.

"Those causes" in *F2* may refer to causes that "change us radically." I am on record as agreeing that, in some cases, it is irrelevant to moral responsibility whether such causes "operate" in one or the other of the two ways mentioned in *F2*. In Mele 1995, commenting on a story like *One Bad Day*, I contend that if the radical reversal at issue were to result from Sally's "passing through a strange, randomly occurring electromagnetic field at the center of the Bermuda Triangle," rather than from the efforts of manipulators, the upshot regarding "psychological autonomy in certain spheres of her life" would be just the same (p. 168); and I would say the same about moral responsibility for particular actions. But this point of mine certainly does not secure the conclusion that my radical reversal suggestions are false. Instead, it identifies a nonintentional way in which what is claimed to be a responsibility-undermining radical reversal of values may, in principle, come about.

I cannot claim anything approaching confidence about exactly what Frankfurt had in mind in the passage I have been discussing. He certainly seems to be thinking that compatibilism—or any compatibilist position that has a fighting chance—commits one to an internalist thesis about moral responsibility for actions. What I am far from sure about is exactly what it is about compatibilism that he thinks generates this result. I have the same uncertainty about Watson and Double, as readers will have noticed.

Some people find the following remark by Frankfurt especially appealing: "We are the sorts of persons we are; and it is what we are, rather than the history of our development, that counts. The fact that someone is a pig warrants treating him like a pig, unless there is reason to believe that in some important way he is a pig against his will and is not acting as he would really prefer to act" (2002, p. 28). Here one reason to withhold such treatment of a "pig" is offered. But I have not seen a persuasive argument for stopping there. If my radical reversal suggestions are on target, there is another reason for withholding treatment of the kind at issue, a reason that includes important facts about how the agent came to be the way he is.

4. TWO WEAK BRANCHES

In earlier chapters, I argued that compatibilists should be conditional externalists. In the present chapter, I examined some lines of thought that are alleged to support the thesis that compatibilists are committed to internalism or should embrace internalism, and I have argued that they are unpersuasive.

The lines of thought I examined branched in two different directions. On one branch, there is the idea that if manipulation of the sort involved in my radical reversal stories were to get an agent off the hook, it would do so only if it includes *deterministic* causation of crucial psychological events or states, in which case determinism would be the real culprit. This idea was found wanting.

On the other branch are some no-difference claims. I compared premise 2 of the argument about Ernie—its no-difference premise—with analogous claims about agents in radical reversal scenarios. The analogous claims were these:

> *B2*. Concerning moral responsibility for the actions at issue, there is no significant difference between the way Sally comes to have the values on which she acts in *One Bad Day* and any of the ways in which unmanipulated human beings come to have such values in a deterministic world.

C2. Concerning their moral responsibility specifically for their good deeds and nothing else, there is no significant difference between the way Chuck comes to have the values on which he acts in *One Good Day* and any of the ways in which unmanipulated human beings come to have such values in a deterministic world.

An adequate defense of these claims—or of parallel claims about the modified versions of *One Bad Day* discussed here—would support the rejection of the conditional externalist view I have been advancing. But I have not found such a defense of them in the lines of thought examined here. Of course, I have not shown that no convincing defense of them is forthcoming; and I look forward to seeing arguments from compatibilists designed to show that they are true.[9]

Chapter 5

Bullet Biting and Beyond

As I see it, compatibilists who reject even the modest externalist theses I have been defending in this book seem to be stuck biting some extremely hard bullets. A question about bullet biting is this chapter's focus. It is roughly this: When should compatibilists about moral responsibility bite the bullet in responding to stories used in arguments for incompatibilism about moral responsibility (or in arguments for theses that typical compatibilists would reject)? To clarify the question, I need to provide some background on bullet biting. That is the business of Section 1. In the remainder of this chapter, I motivate a partial answer.

1. BACKGROUND

Suppose Ed sincerely claims that Sally is morally responsible for killing George in *One Bad Day* and I reply that, in sincerely making that claim, Ed is biting the bullet. What am I saying? Three things: First, Ed's claim is counterintuitive; second, Ed himself finds it counterintuitive; third, Ed is sincerely making the claim because he believes that something else he believes commits him to that claim.

I recognize that there are other ways to use "bite the bullet" in philosophical discussions. For example, some people use the expression in a way that does not require the second element. The question I answered is about *my* usage of the expression.

The issue of sincerity merits a brief comment. For a variety of reasons, Ed may insincerely claim that Sally is morally responsible for killing George. For example, perhaps Ed has published alleged sufficient conditions for moral responsibility for actions that commit him to saying that Sally is morally responsible for the killing, and he may be strongly disinclined to admit that he was wrong even though he is inclined to believe that he was wrong. Another possibility features the following possible facts, in addition to his lacking the belief that Sally is morally responsible for the killing: It is very important to Ed to offer a compatibilist analysis of being morally responsible for an action, he believes that he lacks the patience to figure out how to do that in a way that lets Sally off the hook, and he wants to avoid seeming to shirk his philosophical responsibilities. When the claim about Sally at issue is insincere, there is at most the appearance of bullet biting. (For the record: I have only purely hypothetical philosophers in mind here. Anyone who were to take these remarks personally would be mistaken in so doing.)

2. BITING BULLETS ON BAD DAYS AND GOOD DAYS

Why might someone bite the bullet on Sally in *One Bad Day* (if the claim that Sally is morally responsible for killing George is counterintuitive)? One possibility is that the bullet biter believes that it follows from compatibilism itself about moral responsibility for actions (or this together with some propositions that are known to be true) that if Chuck is morally responsible for killing Don, then Sally is morally responsible for killing George. I examined some unpersuasive arguments for theses of this kind in Chapter 4, and I know of no superior arguments for them. Furthermore, as I explained in Chapter 2, compatibilists are in a position to distinguish among different causal routes to the collections of values agents have at a time and to provide principled grounds for holding that distinct routes to two type-identical collections of values may be such that one and only one of those routes blocks moral responsibility for a pertinent action.

As far as I can see, there is no need for compatibilists (*qua* compatibilists) to bite the bullet on Sally. Of course, some people who claim that Sally is morally responsible for killing George might not see themselves as biting the bullet. They may have the intuition that Sally is morally responsible for this, or they may at least lack the contrary intuition. People who differ in their intuitions (or lack thereof) about Sally's killing of George may try to persuade each other that they are making an error. I have explained why I believe Sally is not morally responsible for the killing, and I continue to be willing to entertain arguments to the contrary.

I turn now to *One Good Day*. Suppose I am right in thinking that it is counterintuitive that Chuck is morally responsible for his good behavior in that story. Are compatibilists who agree with me about this committed to biting the bullet on Chuck simply in virtue of being compatibilists?

Here is *NFMR* from Chapter 3:

> An agent does not freely *A* and is not morally responsible for *A*-ing if the following is true: (1) For years and until manipulators got their hands on him, his system of values was such as to preclude his acquiring even a desire to perform an action of type *A*, much less an intention to perform an action of that type; (2) he was morally responsible for having a long-standing system of values with that property; (3) by means of very recent manipulation to which he did not consent and for which he is not

> morally responsible, his system of values was suddenly and radically transformed in such a way as to render *A*-ing attractive to him during *t*; and (4) the transformation ensures either (*a*) that although he is able during *t* intentionally to do otherwise than *A* during *t*, the only values that contribute to that ability are products of the very recent manipulation and are radically unlike any of his erased values (in content or in strength) or (*b*) that, owing to his new values, he has at least a Luther-style "inability" during *t* intentionally to do otherwise than *A* during *t*.

If *NFMR* is true, Chuck is not morally responsible for the good deeds featured in *One Good Day*. Does this upshot falsify compatibilism about moral responsibility?

If a convincing argument for the following claim were to be offered, compatibilists would be right to worry about the upshot in question:

> *ND*. The differences between Chuck's and Sally's causal histories are irrelevant to whether either agent is morally responsible for his or her good deeds.

If, regarding Chuck's and Sally's moral responsibility for their good actions, there are any important differences between these two agents, those differences lie in their histories. So if the historical differences make no difference and Chuck is not morally responsible for his good deeds, the same is true of Sally. Suppose that Sally's and Chuck's world is deterministic. If Sally is not morally responsible for any of her good deeds in her deterministic world, why would any agent in a deterministic world be morally responsible for anything he or she does? What is the problem with Sally? Now, an incompatibilist can claim that *ND* is true on the grounds that a certain similarity between Chuck's and Sally's causal histories—that they are both deterministic—entails that neither is morally responsible for anything: The differences do not matter. But, of course, no compatibilist would take this line. A compatibilist argument for *ND* may take its lead from Harry Frankfurt's remark, quoted earlier, that "We are inevitably fashioned and sustained, after all, by circumstances over which we have no control" (2002, p. 28). But I have already replied to that thought and to related claims by Richard Double and Gary Watson (see Chapter 4). In the absence of a convincing compatibilist argument for *ND* (and related theses that would yield symmetrical moral-responsibility verdicts about Chuck's and Sally's good deeds), compatibilists who find it intuitive that Chuck is not morally responsible for his good deeds in *One Good Day* have little reason to bite the bullet on Chuck. They can endorse their intuition and remain compatibilists.

3. WHAT ABOUT ERNIE?

My guiding question in this chapter, as I have said, is about when, if ever, compatibilists should bite the bullet in responding to stories used in arguments for incompatibilism about moral responsibility (or in arguments for theses that typical compatibilists would reject). The manipulation stories discussed so far in this chapter feature radical reversals in agents' values. In this section, I take up my original-design story about Ernie and an argument about Ernie that I set out (without endorsing it) in Chapter 4. I repeat the argument here. This time it has a name for ease of reference. I call it *ZAM*.

1. Ernie is not morally responsible for anything he does.
2. Concerning moral responsibility of the beings into whom the zygotes develop, there is no significant difference between

the way Ernie's zygote comes to exist and the way any normal human zygote comes to exist in a deterministic world.

3. So in no possible deterministic world in which a human being develops from a normal human zygote is that human being morally responsible for anything he or she does.

Some people who endorse premise 1 will sincerely report that the premise expresses an intuition they have about Ernie's story. Agnes is such a person. She had self-identified as an agnostic about compatibilism until she encountered Ernie's story. Intuitions about stories are caused. Their causes include features of the stories and features of the people who have the intuitions. What feature of the story might be doing the most work for Agnes? Perhaps the fact that just by assembling the atoms of Ernie's zygote as she does and implanting them in Mary when she does, Diana intentionally brings it about and intentionally ensures that Ernie will do $A_1 \ldots A_n$, where that is a complete, ordered list of Ernie's actions. Let that be a working hypothesis.

Now, this fact—fact *F*—distinguishes Ernie from normal human agents in deterministic worlds. But does this difference between Ernie and the others have a bearing on whether they (that is, the others and Ernie) have or lack moral responsibility for actions? Might this difference support asymmetrical moral-responsibility judgments about Ernie and (some of) the others? This brings us to premise 2. I repeat a point I made in Chapter 4. A defense of premise 2 might begin with the question how it can matter for the purposes of moral responsibility whether, in a deterministic world, a zygote with *Z*'s exact constitution was produced by a supremely intelligent agent with Diana's effective intentions or instead in the way zygotes are normally produced. Imagine a deterministic world *W** that is a lot like the one at issue, *W*, but in which *Z* comes into being in Mary in the normal way and at the same time. It is conceivable that, in *W**, throughout his life, Mary's child, Bernie, does exactly what Ernie does in *W*, down to the smallest detail (with the exception about check signing and the like mentioned earlier). Suppose that this is so, and suppose that Ernie and Bernie have matching "compatibilist-friendly agential structures," to hark back to the discussion in Chapter 3 of some of Michael McKenna's work. Then, a proponent of *ZAM* might contend that, given the additional facts that, in both worlds, the featured agent has no say about what causes *Z*, no say about the rest of the universe at that time, and no say about what the laws of nature are, the cross-world difference in what caused *Z* does not support any cross-world difference in moral responsibility.[1] In the same vein, a proponent of *ZAM* might be impressed by the thought that everything done by Ernie and Bernie is part of the unfolding of their initial conditions—that they are on equal footing on that score.

Recall the claim, discussed in Chapter 4, that if the brainwashing involved in Sally's story gets her off the hook for killing George, it does so only if it *deterministically causes* crucial psychological events or states. I argued that this claim is unwarranted, using an indeterministic scenario in which the open alternatives were Sally's doing what the brainwashers wanted her to do and Sally's breaking down instead. Suppose that Agnes believes that fact *F* justifies premise 1 and she asserts that premise 2 is true. Should a similar move here persuade her that her belief about fact *F* is false or that she should take back her claim about the second premise?

Imagine, if you can, an indeterministic version of Ernie's story in which *F* is false because, on some occasions, there was a chance that instead of performing an action on the list, Ernie would break down and not act at all (see Kearns 2012, pp. 384–86). When Agnes hears the story, she sincerely reports that here too she has the intuition that Ernie is not morally responsible for anything he does. This is compatible with fact *F* being among the causes of her intuition about Ernie in the original story and with fact *F* justifying her belief that Ernie is not morally responsible for anything he does in that story. Furthermore, Agnes does not claim that what Diana does in the original story gets Ernie off the hook only if it *deterministically* causes what it causes. She believes the deterministic nature of the causation is dispensable—at least, after she contemplates the modified story about Ernie. But she does not budge on premise 2. Her reason for assenting to that premise is that she cannot see how the difference between Ernie's origin (in *W*) and the origin of a normal human zygote like the one that grew into Bernie in deterministic world *W** can make a difference regarding their moral responsibility for what they do. That she regards Ernie as nonresponsible in the indeterministic story too has no bearing on this reason.[2]

John Fischer spins a collection of stories in which Ernie is not designed but his parents have various intentions before a momentous sex act (2011, pp. 267–68). In one story, they intend to avoid pregnancy but fail to do so; in another, they intend to have a baby; in a third, they intend their intercourse to "lead to Ernie's performing *A* and bringing about *E* 30 years hence" (p. 268); and so on. Each story is set in a deterministic world, and in each Ernie satisfies conditions many compatibilists deem sufficient for moral responsibility. Fischer contends that "if we start with" his scenarios, "we get the conclusion that the mental states and intentions of the distal creators of the zygote are irrelevant to Ernie's subsequent moral responsibility," but if we start with my story about Ernie "we can come to quite the opposite conclusion" (p. 269).

If we believe that the intentions of Ernie's parents are irrelevant to Ernie's moral responsibility in Fischer's stories, should we also believe that Diana's intentions are irrelevant to his moral responsibility in my story? Agnes is still on stage. Let us ask her.

Agnes invites us to recall fact *F*: Just by assembling the atoms of Ernie's zygote as she does and implanting them in Mary when she does, Diana *intentionally* brings it about and *intentionally* ensures that

Ernie does $A_1 \ldots A_n$, where that is a complete, ordered list of Ernie's actions. She then makes two points. First, Diana's guiding intention is relevant to her intentionally bringing it about and intentionally ensuring that Ernie does $A_1 \ldots A_n$; in the absence of that intention, she would not have done these things. Second, in none of Fischer's stories do the parents seem to have the power to intentionally bring it about and intentionally ensure that Ernie performs all the actions he ends up performing.

Obviously, we are in no position to *deduce* the irrelevance (to Ernie's moral responsibility) of Diana's master intention from the irrelevance (to this) of Ernie's parents' intentions in Fischer's stories. If there is a compelling argument from the irrelevance of the latter to the irrelevance of the former, it is inductive. But the two points Agnes makes cast serious doubt on the induction. In any case, Agnes is not moved at all by Fischer's worry. As she sees things, fact *F* justifies the judgment that Ernie is not morally responsible for anything he does in my story; and there is no counterpart fact in Fischer's stories. That is, the following is false: Just by *X*-ing (fill in *X* as you please), Ernie's parents intentionally bring it about and intentionally ensure that Ernie does $A_1 \ldots A_n$, where that is a complete, ordered list of Ernie's actions.

Anyone who distinguishes intentionally bringing it about that Q and intentionally ensuring that Q happens from merely bringing Q about (as one hoped or perhaps intended to do) understands this last point. But a brief comment on the point might be useful for some readers. Lydia has never fired a gun, and her eyesight is terrible. She has been led to believe that the gun she is holding is loaded with special bull's-eye-seeking bullets and that all she needs to do to ensure that she hits a distant bull's-eye is to point the gun in the direction of the target and pull the trigger. In fact, the bullets are quite ordinary; there is nothing special about them. Lydia intends to hit the bull's-eye by pointing the gun in the general direction of the target and pulling the trigger. Amazingly, as luck would have it, she hits the bull's-eye. She then fires another 200 rounds at it, using the same strategy, and never comes close. We conclude that she has no native skill at target shooting. Obviously, and as any competent action theorist will tell you, Lydia's hitting the bull's-eye was too much a matter of luck (or deficient control over the success of her attempt) to count as an intentional action; and nothing she did counts as intentionally ensuring that she hit the target. So far, John and Mary's success in bringing it about that Ernie *A*-s thirty years later—say, at noon on April 1—resembles Lydia's success in hitting the bull's-eye. It is clear why Agnes sees no counterpart to fact *F* in Fischer's stories.

John Fischer reported in correspondence that he meant one of his stories about Ernie to be much more similar to my story about Ernie than it seems to be. A good way to generate such a story starts by bestowing on Fischer's John and Mary knowledge that is just as impressive as Diana's. They will achieve certain of their goals if they have a child who lives a long, active life and does $A_1 \ldots A_n$, where that is a complete, ordered list of that person's actions. And they deduce from their perfect knowledge of the present condition of their deterministic universe and the laws of nature that if they have sex at a certain time a few months later, arrange to have the child adopted at birth, and never interfere with him, he will do $A_1 \ldots A_n$. They execute their plan, and things happen exactly as they knew they would. The child is named Ernie, of course, and his actions perfectly match those of my Ernie. (Like Diana, John and Mary may be stipulated to be insane and to have no grasp of morality.)[3]

How might Agnes respond to this story? In this story, John and Mary have and successfully exercise the power to intentionally bring it about and intentionally ensure that Ernie does $A_1 \ldots A_n$. This fact may incline Agnes to see Ernie as John and Mary's tool for bringing about what they intend him to bring about and as lacking, for that reason, moral responsibility for his actions. And that inclination may understandably be strengthened by filling in details. Suppose, for example, that Ernie's behavior is a lot like that of Bernie Madoff and that John and Mary's purpose in producing Ernie was to ensure that a certain large collection of people would suffer a great deal of hardship.

It would not be surprising if Agnes's intuition about Ernie's moral responsibility in this new John and Mary story were very similar to her intuition about this in my Diana story. Indeed, the new John and Mary story is similar to a story in which the couple learns that they are incapable of producing exactly the agent they want by means of sexual intercourse and therefore hire Diana to build just the right zygote for them and implant it in Mary at just the right time. The zygote develops into Ernie, who does $A_1 \ldots A_n$, as planned. He is given up for adoption at birth, and Diana, John, and Mary never interfere with him after that. Presumably, Agnes would have the same intuition about Ernie's moral responsibility in this story as she does in the story involved in *ZAM*.

The next item of business is a comment on a confusion about Agnes's contention that fact *F* justifies the judgment that Ernie is not morally responsible for anything he does. (Here is fact *F* again: Just by assembling the atoms of Ernie's zygote as she does and implanting them in Mary when she does, Diana intentionally brings it about and intentionally ensures that Ernie does $A_1 \ldots A_n$, where that is a complete, ordered list of Ernie's actions.) I have heard it said (and not by John Fischer) that this contention cannot be squared with assent to *ZAM*'s second premise: (2) Concerning moral responsibility of the beings into whom the zygotes develop, there is no significant difference between the way Ernie's zygote comes to exist and the way any normal human zygote comes to exist in a deterministic world. Why so? Because, I am told, if premise 2 is true, then fact *F* and the intention to which it alludes are *irrelevant* to whether Ernie is morally responsible for anything he does and things irrelevant to this cannot support *ZAM*'s first premise, the premise stating that Ernie is not morally responsible for anything he does.

One way to test this answer to my question is to suppose that fact *F* and the intention to which it alludes are relevant to whether or not Ernie is morally responsible for things he does and to ascertain whether this is compatible with the truth of premise 2. Here is an assumption that I comment on shortly: (*ASR*) If fact *F* is *sufficient* for Ernie's not being morally responsible for anything he does, then it is relevant to whether Ernie is morally responsible for anything he does. Suppose that fact *F* is sufficient for this, as Agnes contends, and that *ASR* is true. Is this compatible with the truth of premise 2? In addition to believing (*a*) that fact *F* is sufficient for Ernie's not being morally responsible for anything he does, Agnes, as a newly persuaded proponent of *ZAM*, also has come to believe (*b*) that being located in a deterministic world is sufficient for an agent's not being morally responsible for anything he does. And notice that *a*, *b*, and premise 2 form a consistent set (in which case *a* and 2 form a consistent pair, of course). (Readers who have doubts about this should try to derive a contradiction from the set.)

Some readers may be helped to see this by attending to the following trio of propositions:

A. Weighing 75 pounds is sufficient for satisfying football league L's 70-pound minimum weight requirement for playing in a league game.
B. Weighing 71 pounds is sufficient for satisfying football league L's 70-pound minimum weight requirement for playing in a league game.
C. Concerning whether or not a child satisfies football league L's 70-pound minimum weight requirement for playing in a league game, there is no significant difference between weighing 75 pounds and weighing 71 pounds.

This trio is plainly a consistent set. A reminder might also help: By "no significant difference" in premise 2, I mean no difference that would warrant asymmetrical verdicts about pertinent actions (Chapter 4, Section 1). Similarly, in C, "no significant difference" means no difference that would warrant asymmetrical verdicts about whether the 75 pounders and the 71 pounders satisfy the minimum weight requirement.[4]

Assumption *ASR* connects the alleged sufficiency of fact *F* for Ernie's nonresponsibility to the issue of relevance raised by the alleged problem under consideration. Is *ASR* true? It is not a general truth that if *x* is sufficient for *y*, then *x* is relevant to whether *y* is true. On a common conception of sufficiency, the fact that Joe is bored is sufficient for the truth of any necessary truth—for example, "Whatever is blue is blue." But the fact that Joe is bored has no particular relevance to whether this proposition is true. Notably, the fact about Joe does not provide any support for—or any grounds for believing—this proposition. However, the connection Agnes claims to exist between fact *F* and Ernie's nonresponsibility is different. She contends that fact *F* provides support for the claim that Ernie is not morally responsible for anything he does—indeed, support strong enough to justify acceptance of this proposition about Ernie. And if fact *F* does provide support of this kind for this proposition, it is relevant to whether the proposition is true. The take-home message here is that the truth of Agnes's claim that fact *F* justifies the judgment that Ernie is not morally responsible for anything he does is compatible with the truth of *ZAM*'s second premise. Agnes can consistently believe both that her claim about fact *F* is true and, for example, that there is no difference between Ernie and Bernie that would warrant asymmetrical verdicts about their moral responsibility for their actions. Her reflection on Ernie's story may lead her to believe that Ernie is not morally responsible for anything he does, and her careful search for a difference between Ernie and any agent who develops from a normal human zygote in a deterministic world that would justify asymmetrical verdicts about their moral responsibility for actions may turn up nothing that she finds credible. In the end, she may—without contradiction—assent to both of *ZAM*'s premises, and she may draw *ZAM*'s conclusion. Whether those premises are in fact true is another matter.

To be sure, there is a difference between being designed in the way Ernie was and not being designed. Agnes grants that this difference may be important or significant for some purposes. Her claim about this difference is that it does not have the significance at issue in *ZAM*'s second premise—that is, that it does not warrant asymmetrical verdicts about moral responsibility.

It is time to leave Agnes behind—along with all the Ernies except the one at issue in *ZAM*. If it is assumed that premise 2 of *ZAM* is true, what should *compatibilists* say about premise 1? They should say that it is false, as I observed in Mele 2006 (p. 193). Compatibilists believe that there are morally responsible human agents in some deterministic possible worlds and that the zygotes of many of them come to be in the normal way. Given their compatibilism, Ernie's properties as an agent, and the assumption that premise 2 is true, they should claim that Ernie is morally responsible for at least some of what he does. Many compatibilists may regard this claim as plausible and not see themselves as biting the bullet on Ernie.

Sometimes authors craft arguments with the intention or hope of persuading every reasonable person who reads them. I certainly do not have that hope for *ZAM*. As I mentioned in Mele 2006 (pp. 193–94), I myself am not persuaded by the zygote argument, a close cousin of *ZAM* that includes similar premises. I am not convinced that Ernie is not morally responsible for anything he does. (But I also am not convinced that he is.) So why did I spin Ernie's story and offer the zygote argument for consideration? Because the story and argument seem to me to help crystallize an incompatibilist worry about compatibilism (see McKenna 2009, pp. 25–26), because I hoped to prompt instructive compatibilist responses to that worry, and because the story and argument might shed some light on why someone might be agnostic about compatibilism, as I am.

Fischer reports that "it is often said that the Zygote Argument and similar arguments display the 'price' of compatibilism—they indicate what a compatibilist must be prepared to accept, where this is somehow more 'philosophically expensive' than compatibilism was antecedently thought to be" (2011, p. 271). He does not see these arguments as raising the price of compatibilism; and he asks, rhetorically, "How could it increase the cost of compatibilism to show that a compatibilist must accept that an agent is morally responsible in a scenario that is no different than an ordinary situation in which there is no special reason to call into question the agent's moral responsibility?" But Fischer grants that his opponent can claim that "the Zygote Argument . . . shows that an ordinary situation is just as worrisome as a scenario that is indeed *prima facie* problematic (the Diana scenario)," and he says that at this point a "dialectical stalemate" has been reached.

I mention these remarks by Fischer because of their connection with the topic of bullet biting. Seasoned compatibilists like Fischer may not see themselves as biting the bullet at all in claiming that my Ernie is morally responsible for some of what he does; they may not see their claim as at all counterintuitive. Indeed, they may find it highly plausible and even intuitive. Even so, many of their opponents may regard the claim as highly counterintuitive (see Todd 2013).

What might account for this difference in attitudes? Might it be that significantly different conceptions of moral responsibility (for actions) are at work here? If so, each side might try to explain to the other why the other side's conception is actually a misconception. Fischer refers to arguments for compatibilism in his discussion of my zygote argument (2011, pp. 267–68). One tack for a compatibilist to take is to argue that the power of his or her arguments for compatibilism is such that any rational person who gives those arguments a fair hearing will see that, even if the claim that Ernie is morally responsible for some of what he does strikes one as very counterintuitive, it is nevertheless true.[5]

Imagine, if you can, a rational person, Réka, who finds *ZAM* more persuasive than the collection of arguments for compatibilism. How might she proceed? One thing she might notice is that Ernie's story may be viewed as an attempted counterexample to compatibilism about moral responsibility in ordinary human beings, or at least to sufficient conditions for moral responsibility that compatibilists have proposed. Ernie—at least with explicit additions that are in line with the spirit of my story (for example, he often "identifies himself with the springs of his actions" [Frankfurt 1988, p. 54])—easily satisfies any compatibilist set of proposed sufficient conditions for moral responsibility that Réka or I have seen. And even so, he strikes Réka as lacking moral responsibility. Taking her lead from Patrick Todd (2013, pp. 194–95, 199), Réka reports that it is obvious to her that a being like Ernie whose every action is "predetermined" by a powerful designer is not morally responsible for what he does and even so, she says, many of Ernie's actions satisfy conditions compatibilists claim to be sufficient for moral responsibility. She also claims that compatibilists have no resources for avoiding the counterexample in the case of beings like us, because, when it comes to moral responsibility, there is no significant difference between the way Ernie's zygote comes to exist and the way any normal human zygote comes to exist in a deterministic world (see *ZAM*, premise 2).

Réka may strike you as naive. She seems not to recognize that even though it seems obvious to her that Ernie is not morally responsible for anything, there are people who confidently assert that Ernie is morally responsible for some of his actions and are quite willing to try to persuade her that this is so. But, despite her naivete, Réka is relevant to the issue about cost that Fischer raised. Seasoned compatibilists should not be expected to be stunned—or even budged—by my story about Diana and Ernie. The cost lies elsewhere. Naturally, typical compatibilists sometimes try to persuade their non-compatibilist readers (including incompatibilists, agnostics, and people who have never heard of compatibilism) that compatibilism is true. Ernie's story and *ZAM* may make this harder to do than it would otherwise be in the case of at least some readers who had never contemplated stories like Ernie's (see McKenna 2009, p. 26). I return to this point shortly.

Elsewhere, I have suggested that incompatibilist believers in moral responsibility for action should try to do more than they have to explain how human agents in indeterministic worlds can be morally responsible for some of their actions (Mele 2013c). In this connection, I highlighted an analogy with defenses and theodicies in the philosophy of religion. Defenses are critiques of arguments designed to show that the pain and suffering in the world are incompatible with the existence of a perfect God; theodicies are attempts to explain why a perfect God would allow all the bad stuff. Incompatibilist believers in moral responsibility tend to concentrate on rebutting arguments against their position. This is understandable. But the more difficult project of explaining how moral responsibility is possible when typical specifically incompatibilist requirements for it are satisfied is an important one. A similar observation applies to compatibilist believers in human moral responsibility. They too tend to concentrate, understandably, on rebutting arguments against their position. But convincing arguments for such things as compatibilism itself (about moral responsibility for actions) or the truth of the claim that Ernie is morally responsible for some of his actions would certainly be desirable, and that ambitious project would seem to merit more attention than it has received. I, for one, would love to see an argument that convinces me that Ernie is morally responsible for some of what he does and moves me to abandon my agnosticism in favor of compatibilism.

If I have strayed from the topic of bullet biting, it is time to get back on track. Biting the bullet on a story, according to the account I offered in Section 1, has three elements: sincerely making a counterintuitive claim about the story, finding that claim counterintuitive oneself, and sincerely making the claim because one believes that something else one believes commits one to making it. My description of the first element should prompt a question: Counterintuitive to whom? Possible answers include the following: everyone, all people capable of having intuitions about the matter, most people, and some people. This list of possible answers is far from complete, of course. The following answer would allow me to get by with a two-element account of bullet biting: counterintuitive to the person making the claim. The resulting account is attractive in some ways. But it leaves us with a question raised by the second element in my three-element account. How are we to know whether a person making a claim regards it as counterintuitive? I suppose that we can just take his or her word for it. But entertaining that option should make us wonder how much it matters whether some individual or other—including me, of course—has or lacks a certain intuition about a case.

Some readers may not be familiar with the malady known as intuition deficit disorder (*IDD*). In one of its manifestations, people who suffer from it are blind to counterexamples to their theories about things, except when the counterexamples are widely recognized to be real-world events, states, or beings. Philosophers have been known to test their own tentative analyses of things by attempting to invent counterexamples to those analyses, and they have been known to adjust their provisional analyses in light of their intuitions about cases. Sometimes, after years spent considering a wide range of cases and refining their provisional analyses in light of their intuitions, they wind up not only with an analysis they like but also with *IDD*. If someone has this malady, the fact that he or she lacks certain intuitions does not count for much.

It is possible that I myself have *IDD* in the sphere of moral responsibility (not to mention other spheres). I have strong intuitions that Sally is not morally responsible for killing George in *One Bad Day* and my spin-off stories about that killing and that Chuck is not morally responsible for the good deeds featured in *One Good Day*; but I have neither the intuition that Ernie is not morally responsible for anything he does nor the intuition that he is morally responsible for some of what he does.[6] When I take a third-person, diagnostic stance toward myself and ask why that is, a certain observation quickly comes to mind. As I have explained, I see no good reason to believe that compatibilism about moral responsibility (or this together with propositions known to be true) yields the verdict that either Sally or Chuck is morally responsible for their pertinent deeds in these radical reversal stories, but I am inclined to believe that the combination of compatibilism and a popular view of laws of nature yields the verdict that Ernie is morally responsible for some of his actions.[7] Although I have never endorsed compatibilism, I have expressed my agnosticism about it. So things are falling into place for me from my third-person, diagnostic perspective. Perhaps I lack the nonresponsibility intuition about Ernie because I am biased by my avowal of agnosticism about compatibilism.

When philosophers tell me that they lack an intuition that *p* that seemingly conflicts with a philosophical position in which they are heavily invested, I am not terribly surprised. If I succeed in showing them that the deepest parts of their position are compatible with the truth of *p*, then if lots of people claim to have strong intuitions that *p*, these philosophers might be inclined to modify their position in such a way as to accommodate *p* or leave *p* open. Both in this book and elsewhere, I have tried to do this favor for compatibilists who have endorsed theses that commit them to holding that Sally is morally responsible for killing George in *One Bad Day* and the spin-off stories or that Chuck is morally responsible for his good deeds in *One Good Day*.

Regarding Ernie's story, I have less to offer compatibilists. As I made clear in Mele 2006 (pp. 190–93) and repeated here, I certainly do not expect the story to move seasoned compatibilists to reject compatibilism, and I myself lack the intuition that Ernie is not morally responsible for anything he does. Fischer argues that the zygote argument is "not decisive" (2011, p. 272), and I obviously agree. But to return to Fischer's "price" metaphor, I believe that many compatibilists who take it to be important to persuade non-compatibilists that compatibilism is true do have a price to pay. For compatibilists who accept or are open to a view of laws of nature in light of which Ernie's story is coherent (see note 7) and who accept premise 2 of *ZAM*, the price is whatever it costs to produce arguments for the truth of compatibilism powerful enough to persuade many potential recruits from the non-compatibilist ranks that Ernie is morally responsible for some of what he does. And how is this price to be measured? In terms of time and effort, of course.

4. HARD-LINING AND SOFT-LINING

In a straightforward style of manipulation argument against a proposed compatibilist sufficient condition for an agent's being morally responsible for an action—or against compatibilism about moral responsibility in general—one premise is an assertion about an action performed in a deterministic world by an imaginary manipulated agent. Call the agent Manny. The assertion is that Manny is not morally responsible for *A*-ing. Call this the *Manny premise*. Whether a Manny premise would be deemed true or false by most compatibilists depends on the story spun about Manny, of course. If, in a deterministic world, a Girl Scout manipulates Manny by flashing a subliminal "cookies!" message that gives him a desire to buy some cookies and he can easily resist the desire (in some respectable compatibilist sense of "can") but buys a box of cookies nonetheless, competent compatibilists would definitely view the manipulation as consistent with his being morally responsible for buying the cookies.

What happens next in a manipulation argument of the kind at issue depends on how ambitious the argument's author is. The author might argue that Manny satisfies all alleged sets of conceptually or metaphysically sufficient conditions for morally responsible action ever proposed by compatibilists. If that is true of Manny and the Manny premise is true, then Manny's story is a counterexample to all of these alleged sets of sufficient conditions. Of course, even if the story is a counterexample to all this, it does not follow that incompatibilism about moral responsibility is true. Perhaps the story is not a counterexample to some superior candidate for being a set of conceptually or metaphysically sufficient conditions for moral responsibility that is consistent with the truth of determinism and has not yet been proposed by compatibilists. Perhaps Manny fails to satisfy some conditions in this set. A bolder incompatibilist may seek to close this gap by arguing for the following premise: Concerning moral responsibility, there is no significant difference between Manny's *A*-ing and any candidate for an action for which its agent is morally responsible in a deterministic world.[8] This a *no-difference* premise.

This bolder incompatibilist is arguing directly for incompatibilism about moral responsibility rather than against alleged sets of conceptually or metaphysically sufficient conditions for moral responsibility that compatibilists have proposed. This bold theorist is arguing, in part, as follows:

1. (Manny premise) Manny is not morally responsible for *A*-ing.
2. (No-difference premise) Concerning moral responsibility, there is no significant difference between Manny's *A*-ing and any candidate for an action for which an agent is morally responsible in a deterministic world.
3. So no candidate for an action for which its agent is morally responsible in a deterministic world is an action for which the agent is morally responsible; in short, compatibilism about moral responsibility is false.

I mentioned that whether most compatibilists would regard a particular Manny premise as true depends on the details of the story about the manipulated agent. The same is true of the no-difference premise. Whether compatibilists would accept the claim that, concerning moral responsibility, there is no significant difference between Manny's *A*-ing and any candidate for an action for which its agent is morally responsible in a deterministic world depends on the details of the story about Manny's *A*-ing.

Michael McKenna refers to a rebuttal of a premise like 1 as a "hard-line" response to a manipulation argument and a rebuttal of a premise like 2 as a "soft-line" response (2008, p. 143). He rightly observes that "there is no one-size-fits-all compatibilist reply" to arguments of the sort at issue, because "which premise a compatibilist should reject depends" on the stories or cases used to support the first premise (p. 143). In McKenna's terminology, what I have been arguing is that a soft-line reply to arguments whose Manny premise is supported by such radical reversal stories as *One Good Day* and *One Bad Day* is much more plausible than a hard-line response to them, even if a soft-line reply to *ZAM* is not a viable option.[9] If Chuck in *One Good Day* and Sally in *One Bad Day* are not morally responsible for the deeds featured in those stories even though their unmanipulated counterparts are morally responsible for deeds of the same kind, then conditional externalism is true, and so is an externalist thesis that extends well beyond what is needed to accommodate asymmetrical judgments about Van and Ike, the drunk drivers discussed in Chapter 1. I return to this point in Chapter 6.

5. A BRIEF COMMENTARY ON ZYGOTE-STYLE ARGUMENTS

My zygote argument (Mele 2006, p. 189) has generated a great deal of discussion. The argument appears in Mele 2006 in, as I put it there, "skeleton form" (p. 189).[10] It is similar in form to *ZAM*. When I introduced *ZAM* in Chapter 4 (an unnamed argument at that point), I pointed out that the argument is enthymematic (as is the zygote argument). A comment on this feature of *ZAM* is appropriate here.

To spare readers the trouble of looking back for *ZAM*, here it is again:

1. Ernie is not morally responsible for anything he does.
2. Concerning moral responsibility of the beings into whom the zygotes develop, there is no significant difference between the way Ernie's zygote comes to exist and the way any normal human zygote comes to exist in a deterministic world.
3. So in no possible deterministic world in which a human being develops from a normal human zygote is that human being morally responsible for anything he or she does.

As it stands, *ZAM* is not valid. Even if 1 and 2 are true, the truth of 2 is compatible with there being differences between Ernie and some normally produced human agents in possible deterministic worlds in virtue of which these other agents, unlike Ernie, are morally responsible for some of what they do. An easy way to see this is to consider the proposal that Ernie does not have a robust enough collection of nonhistorical agential features to be morally responsible for actions he performs whereas some other normally produced human agents in possible deterministic worlds do. Readers who recall Ernie's impressive features and recognize that they far outstrip what various compatibilists deem sufficient for moral responsibility for actions are likely to regard this proposal as preposterous. But the point now is that *ZAM*'s premises themselves do not contradict this proposal and therefore do not entail 3. In short, *ZAM*, as it stands, is not valid.

For my purposes, this point about *ZAM* (and the zygote argument) is no cause for worry. My reason for formulating the argument skeleton or sketch as I did was to focus attention on what I wanted to be salient: the nonresponsibility claim about Ernie and the idea that, as far as responsibility goes, normally produced human agents in possible deterministic worlds are no better off than an agent who was designed in the way Ernie was. Just as Ernie has no say about the conditions in place at the time of his conception and no say about the laws of nature (setting aside Humeanism about laws of nature), neither do they; and everything the agents—Ernie and the others—do later may be viewed as part of the unfolding of their initial conditions. These two planks in the argument are what have dominated attention in the literature on zygote-style arguments, and rightly so. My primary aim in presenting zygote-style arguments has been to motivate compatibilists to explain why one or the other of those planks ought to be rejected.

To readers who would like to see a valid version of *ZAM*, I offer the following, which I dub *ZAM2*:

1. Ernie is not morally responsible for anything he does.
2a. If Ernie is not morally responsible for anything he does, no human being who develops from a normal human zygote in a

deterministic world is morally responsible for anything he or she does.

3. So in no possible deterministic world in which a human being develops from a normal human zygote is that human being morally responsible for anything he or she does.

ZAM2 obscures the point featured in *ZAM*'s second premise. The point can be recaptured in an argument for 2a. An argument for 2a may be composed of an argument for 2 together with an argument that closes the gap left open by 2. A fully developed version of *ZAM2* would include arguments for the premises that do not presuppose incompatibilism about moral responsibility for actions.[11]

Chapter 6

Wrapping Things Up

In Chapter 1, I invited readers to imagine that they have agreed to construct an analysis of "*S* is morally responsible for *A*-ing," where *S* is a placeholder for any possible agent and *A* is a placeholder for any possible action. As I mentioned, I do not undertake this analytical task in this book. Even so, attention to how someone might go about constructing such an analysis will prove instructive.

The content of one's analysis will depend, among other things, on one's position on compatibilism about moral responsibility for actions. A compatibilist about this will try to construct an analysis the conditions of which are satisfiable in a deterministic possible world, and an incompatibilist will try to construct an incompatibilist analysis. I have had little to say about incompatibilism in this book and even less to say about the bearing of manipulation on the project of constructing an incompatibilist analysis of moral responsibility for actions. The bearing of manipulation on this project is the topic of Section 1. In subsequent sections, I branch out.

1. MORAL RESPONSIBILITY AND INDETERMINISM

I have already discussed the issue of moral responsibility for actions in a couple of explicitly indeterministic scenarios—an indeterministic version of *One Bad Day* (Chapters 4 and 5) and an indeterministic version of my story about Ernie (Chapter 5). In the present section, I return to an indeterministic story about manipulation that I use in Mele 2006 to illustrate a problem for Robert Kane's libertarian view.

Someone might think that indeterminism in an action-producing process is enough to thwart any potential manipulator. Recall (from Chapter 1) Kane's contention that if it is causally undetermined what a particular agent will choose, "no potential controller could manipulate the situation in advance so that the choice necessarily comes out as the controller plans or intends" and that its being the case that an agent is not causally determined to choose what he chooses at *t* therefore "thwarts[s] *any* potential CNC controller" who wishes to control what the agent chooses at *t* (1985, p. 36). As I mentioned in Chapter 1, in cases of CNC control, as Kane understands such control, the manipulator covertly arranges "circumstances beforehand so that the agent wants and desires, and hence chooses and tries, only what the controller intends" (p. 37).

In Mele 2006, I argue that even given indeterminism at the moment of choice, a manipulator may exert enough control over what an agent chooses to preclude the agent's being morally responsible for making the choice he makes (and his making it freely). My argument takes account of Kane's view about free decisions or choices that an agent is morally responsible for in a fundamental way (Kane 1999a, 1999b).[1] Some background on that view helps set the stage for the argument.

Kane's proposed solution to a certain worry about indeterministic luck in cases in which the alternative actions at issue are decisions features the idea that the agent simultaneously tries to make each of two or more competing choices or decisions (1999b).[2] To keep things relatively simple, I focus on a scenario in which only two competing choices are in the running and the agent's options are morally significant. Regarding such cases, Kane claims that because the agent is trying to make each choice, she is morally responsible for whichever of the two choices she makes and makes it freely (pp. 231–40), provided that "she endorse[s] the outcome as something she was trying and wanting to do all along" (p. 233). Obviously, Kane is here proposing a sufficient condition for being morally responsible for a choice and for choosing freely.

Consider the following case from Mele 2006 (p. 52). The setting is indeterministic, and it is at no time determined which choice the agent will make:

> A manipulator compels an agent, Antti, simultaneously to try to choose to *A* and to try to choose to *B*, where *A* and *B* are competing courses of action that, in the absence of manipulation, Antti would abhor performing . . . . The manipulator does not allow Antti to try to choose anything else at the time and . . . the manipulation is such that Antti will endorse either relevant "outcome as something [he] was trying and wanting to do all along."

My assessment of the case is predictable: "The tryings are internally indeterministic, but Antti does not freely try to make the choices he tries to make. Apparently, whatever he chooses, he does not freely choose it—especially when the sort of freedom at issue is the sort most closely associated with moral responsibility" (p. 52).

Imagine a version of Antti's story in which, before he is manipulated, his values, personality, and history are a lot like pre-manipulation Sally's. Add the detail that just as Sally dislikes George, Antti dislikes a pair of neighbors, twin brothers Pekka and Petri, who share a house next to his. In this version of the story, Antti's manipulation is very similar to Sally's in *One Bad Day*. Like Sally, he is given Chuck's nasty values after his own competing values are erased. And right up to the time at which he makes his choice, it is undetermined whether Antti will decide to kill Pekka first, decide to kill Petri first, or suffer a breakdown that prevents him from making any decision at all. Owing to the manipulation, one of these three things will occur. As it happens, Antti decides to kill Pekka first, which is what he proceeds to do.

As I see it, a libertarian who judges that Sally's manipulation is such that she is not morally responsible for killing George in *One Bad Day* should also judge that Antti is not morally responsible for killing Pekka. That, owing to the indeterminism in his story, it was possible for Antti to decide to kill Petri first and possible for him to suffer a breakdown makes no contribution to a credible case for the claim that he differs from manipulated Sally in such a way that he is morally responsible for killing Pekka. And the same goes for the claims that Antti is morally responsible for *deciding* to kill Pekka and for deciding to kill him *first*.[3]

I have just made a point about libertarians who take a certain position on Sally in *One Bad Day*. What about my own view? The considerations I would offer in support of my judgment that Antti is not morally responsible for killing Pekka are of the same kind as the considerations I offered in similar cases that are not explicitly indeterministic. Antti's pre-transformation character was sufficiently good that killing Pekka was not even an option for him; and the combination of this fact with the fact that Antti was morally responsible (to some significant extent) for that character, facts about his history that account for his moral responsibility for that character, facts about his post-manipulation character and associated abilities, and the facts that account for his killing Pekka suffices for his not being morally responsible for killing him. Considerations of the same sort support the further judgments that Antti is not morally responsible for deciding to kill Pekka nor for deciding to kill him first. The bottom line is that the general idea underlying my radical reversal suggestions applies not only to some deterministic cases but also to some explicitly indeterministic ones.

I presented Antti's story in the context of a particular event-causal libertarian view. There are competing libertarian views, including agent-causal views. Suppose Antti has agent-causal power in the story I have told about him. He can agent-cause a decision or intention to kill Pekka first, agent-cause a decision or intention to kill Petri first, or break down. The difference between this agent-causal story about Antti and a parallel event-causal story about him does not support the contention that in the agent-causal story, unlike its event-causal counterpart, Antti is morally responsible for killing Pekka. The same is true of Antti's deciding to kill Pekka and his deciding to kill Pekka first. Agent-causal power is sometimes alleged to be a marvelous thing, but it does not immunize agents who have it against the manipulators at work in my stories.[4] If I am right, both compatibilists and incompatibilists should accommodate my radical reversal suggestions and the general idea underlying them in their attempted analyses of moral responsibility for actions.

2. DIRECT AND INDIRECT MORAL RESPONSIBILITY

As I have mentioned, some philosophers—myself included—distinguish between direct and indirect moral responsibility for actions. If we are right to do so, this is something to be accommodated by a philosopher with the analytical project under discussion. In my usage, as I reported in Chapter 1, an agent is *directly* morally responsible for *A*-ing when and only when he is morally responsible for *A*-ing and his moral responsibility for this is not wholly inherited from his moral responsibility for other things. As I observed, being directly morally responsible for *A*-ing, so construed, is a matter of having at least *some* direct (that is, uninherited) moral responsibility for *A*-ing.

These comments are specifically about the *directness* of direct moral responsibility, of course. What about the whole ball of wax?

Some artists like to make a crude sketch of a painting they are planning before they paint. Suppose that, in one's thinking about what direct moral responsibility for an action might be, one starts with an extremely crude sketch, as follows:

> *CS*. *S* is directly morally responsible for *A*-ing if and only if *S* satisfies all internal and external necessary conditions for this.

In Chapter 1, I characterized an agent's *internal condition* at a time as something specified by the collection of all psychological truths about the agent at the time that are silent on how he came to be as he is at that time. In *CS*, *internal necessary conditions* for being directly morally responsible for *A*-ing are understood to be, first, any such psychological truths about the agent that are necessary for his being directly morally responsible for *A*-ing and, second, the fact that the agent *A*-ed. *External necessary conditions* for being directly morally responsible for *A*-ing are all other necessary conditions for this.

Of course, there is considerable disagreement about what the internal necessary conditions for direct moral responsibility for an action are, and the same goes for external necessary conditions. But if there are any external necessary conditions for direct moral responsibility for an action, an adequate analysis of being directly morally responsible for *A*-ing will need to capture them.

Are there any external necessary conditions for being directly morally responsible for *A*-ing? If I am right, here is one (see *NFMR* in Chapter 3):

> *DMR*. If an agent is directly morally responsible for *A*-ing, then the following is false: (1) for years and until manipulators got their hands on him, his system of values was such as to preclude

> his acquiring even a desire to perform an action of type *A*, much less an intention to perform an action of that type; (2) he was morally responsible for having a long-standing system of values with that property; (3) by means of very recent manipulation to which he did not consent and for which he is not morally responsible, his system of values was suddenly and radically transformed in such a way as to render *A*-ing attractive to him during *t*; and (4) the transformation ensures either (*a*) that although he is able during *t* intentionally to do otherwise than *A* during *t*, the only values that contribute to that ability are products of the very recent manipulation and are radically unlike any of his erased values (in content or in strength) or (*b*) that, owing to his new values, he has at least a Luther-style "inability" during *t* intentionally to do otherwise than *A* during *t*.

I am not saying that *DMR* itself will be part of an adequate analysis of an agent's being directly morally responsible for *A*-ing. Rather, my claim is that an adequate analysis will accommodate various facts for which *DMR* helps to account. For example, it will accommodate the fact that agents such as Chuck in *One Good Day* and Sally in *One Bad Day* are not morally responsible for their featured deeds in those stories. (Obviously, if they are not morally responsible for these deeds, they are not *directly* morally responsible for them.) This fact—or, at least, what I claim to be a fact—can only be accommodated by a necessary condition for moral responsibility for *A*-ing that these agents fail to satisfy for the actions at issue. (Here I am assuming that moral responsibility for actions, including the direct variety, is susceptible to analysis.) Take Chuck in *One Good Day*. If my verdict that he is not morally responsible for helping the Girl Scouts and homeless people is correct even though unmanipulated Sally is directly morally responsible for at least some of her good deeds, it is owing partly to how Chuck came to be the way he is on that day—that is, owing partly to this *historical* and hence *external* matter—that he is not morally responsible for these deeds. Call this point about Chuck and Sally *HCS*. (Notice that I am assuming here that moral responsibility for actions is possible.) Given that Chuck helps the Girl Scouts but is not morally responsible for so doing, he fails to satisfy some necessary condition for being morally responsible for helping them. (After all, if he satisfied all necessary conditions for being morally responsible for helping them, he would be morally responsible for helping them.) So given *HCS*, some necessary condition that Chuck fails to satisfy is an *external* one. If there were no external condition for moral responsibility, then Chuck would be morally responsible for his good deeds in *One Good Day*, just as unmanipulated Sally is for hers.

In Chapter 1, I distinguished between unconditional and conditional varieties of internalism and externalism about moral responsibility for actions. *Unconditional internalism*, again, is the thesis that an agent's internal condition at the relevant time (a time beginning shortly before his *A*-ing begins) and the involvement of that condition in his *A*-ing are relevant to whether he is morally responsible for *A*, and no fact about how he came to be in that condition is relevant. If I am right, my stories about Van and Ike falsify unconditional internalism. The falsity of unconditional internalism is sufficient for the truth of *conditional externalism*, the thesis that agents sometimes are morally responsible for *A* partly because of how they came to be in the internal condition that issues in their *A*-ing; and, more specifically, in these cases, there is another possible way of having come to be in that internal condition such that if they had come to be in that condition in that way, then, holding everything else fixed (except what is entailed by the difference), including the fact that they *A*-ed, they would not have been morally responsible for *A*.

Narrower and broader versions of conditional externalism may be distinguished. According to a very narrow version, conditional externalism is true only in the sphere of wholly inherited moral responsibility for actions. According to a broader version, conditional externalism also is true of some actions for which agents are directly morally responsible. Relevant stories here include *One Good Day* and *Bad Day Modified*. If I am right, Chuck is not morally responsible for any of his good deeds in *One Good Day* even though unmanipulated Sally is directly morally responsible for some similar deeds of hers, and Sally is not morally responsible for killing George in *Bad Day Modified* even though Chuck, in *Bad Chuck*, is directly morally responsible for killing Don.[5] The crucial difference between these pairs of agents is in how they came to be as they are at the relevant times; it is an *external* difference. I have argued that conditional externalism is true and that its truth is not restricted to the narrow sphere of wholly inherited moral responsibility for actions.

3. TONING IT DOWN

Most of my radical reversal stories in this book have been about extremely evil or exceptionally good agents whose moral personalities are turned upside down by manipulators. Is that because I think that only such stories should lead us to accept a conditional externalism that extends to direct moral responsibility for actions? No. I use these stories because I regard them as particularly effective.

I also believe that some stories in which the drama is significantly toned down warrant acceptance of this kind of externalism. Recall the story about Paul, the manipulated father, in Chapter 3. In my view, as I reported, he is not morally responsible for taking out a loan to fund his daughter's education, even though his unmanipulated counterpart, Pat, is morally responsible for doing the same for his own daughter. The next story to be told is comparable to Paul's.

One Generous Day. Rudy is an exceptionally stingy person. Although he is sixty years old and has always been financially well off, Rudy has never donated money to any cause. Nor has he had a desire to do so in the last half century. Even though he never intentionally set out to make himself stingy nor to bolster his stinginess, Rudy wholeheartedly identifies with his stinginess. He views it as entirely reasonable and regards generous people as suckers. If moral responsibility for traits such as stinginess is common in Rudy's world, Rudy is morally responsible for this trait of his. Aside from his extreme stinginess, Rudy is a relatively normal person. Among other things, he is not a criminal, nor is he disposed to take pleasure in other people's suffering. Last night, while he slept, a team of scientists implanted in Rudy a strong (but not irresistible) desire to embark on a project of generous action and a belief that generous behavior is exceptionally good, after erasing all values that would conflict with this new one. When Rudy awakes on a beautiful Saturday morning, his mind is flooded by thoughts of donating money to various worthy causes. He is amazed to find himself thinking about such things; and as he drinks his morning coffee, he mulls the matter over. Rudy concludes that he has finally seen the light about generosity, and he gets on with his day. His first stop is his bank, where Rudy withdraws ten-thousand dollars. By noon, he has bought cookies from a dozen Girl Scouts, made substantial donations at a pair of homeless shelters, and put large wads of cash in several church poor boxes. After lunch, his charitable giving continues for hours—until his cash is gone. Rudy falls asleep that night with a big smile on his face; he is very pleased with the day's activities. Minutes later, the brainwashing is undone. When Rudy awakes the next morning he is extremely upset about having given his money away. He is convinced that he had gone insane for a day, and he schedules an appointment with a psychiatrist.

It will come as no surprise to readers that I have no inclination at all to believe that Rudy deserves moral credit for his charitable deeds. Realizing that if he were morally responsible for these good deeds he would deserve moral credit for them, I judge that Rudy is not morally responsible for these deeds. The change in Rudy is considerably less extensive than the changes in Chuck and Sally in *One Good Day, One Bad Day,* and *Bad Day Modified,* but my reasons for taking the view I do about Rudy are similar to my reasons for contending that Chuck and Sally are not morally responsible for the deeds at issue in those stories. My verdict about *One Generous Day* is supported by the following collection of facts: For many years and until manipulators got their hands on him, Rudy's system of values was such that, despite having many opportunities for generosity, he did not even once desire to perform a charitable deed; he was morally responsible for having the long-standing values at issue, values in light of which charitable giving was not an option for him; by means of very recent manipulation to which he did not consent and for which he is not morally responsible, his system of values was suddenly transformed in such a way as to render charitable deeds very attractive to him; and he performed each of his charitable deeds because of the manipulation. In light of these facts, I see Rudy as not being deserving of moral credit for his charitable deeds.

Thus far in this section, I have toned down the drama along one dimension—the extensiveness of the change wrought by manipulation. I turn now to another dimension.

Consider a variant of *One Good Day* in which the effects of the manipulation last only for an hour but are no less powerful during that time. Chuck spends part of the hour reflecting on his new values while drinking his morning coffee. Then he walks outside and sees a little girl crying because her kitten has climbed a tree and is too frightened to climb back down. Chuck, motivated solely by implanted values, decides to help the child. He climbs the tree, fetches the kitten, and hands it to the girl. Chuck smiles at her and then passes out. A few minutes later, he shakes his head, pulls himself up, and wonders why on Earth he helped the child. He is back to normal—for him. Call this story *One Good Deed.*

Here, what I have toned down is the magnitude of Chuck's good deeds. As I see it, just as Chuck deserves no moral credit for any of his many good deeds in *One Good Day,* he deserves no moral credit for the good deed featured in *One Good Deed.* My reasons for taking this view of things can be inferred from the reasons I offered for my verdict about the former story.

A good-to-bad story like *One Bad Day* can be modified in a similar way. Imagine that the only change in the story is that Sally kills a dog she has found irritating rather than a person. The magnitude of the bad done decreases; but, as I see it, the nonresponsibility verdict remains the same—and for reasons of the same kind that support the verdict that Sally is not morally responsible for killing George. A story in which the drama is reduced along a third dimension appears in the following section.

4. QUESTIONS AND ANSWERS

The present section poses some questions and offers some answers. This is an efficient way to cover some ground.

Question 1. Assume that Mabel, the amazing self-transformer (Chapter 2), is a possible being. How can you say that there's an external necessary condition for being directly morally responsible for *A*-ing when you grant that Mabel can be directly morally responsible for any morally significant action she performs, no matter what lengths manipulators go to in changing her values?

Notice that Mabel's being directly morally responsible for actions is compatible with the truth of *DMR* (see Section 2), an alleged external necessary condition for direct moral responsibility for an action. Actions for which Mabel is directly morally responsible do not falsify the claim that *DMR* is true; they are not counterexamples to *DMR*. They leave standing an alleged *external necessary* condition for direct moral responsibility for actions.[6]

Question 2. Why do you say that you have offered a *negative* historical constraint on moral responsibility? You say that you do not require that a morally responsible agent has an agential history of a certain kind but instead that he *lacks* a certain kind of agential history. But isn't lacking a certain kind of agential history a matter of having an agential history of some other kind?

Consider the first action performed by an instant agent. Until he performs that action, he has not acted; and, by definition, having an agential history at *t* requires having acted before *t*. At the time at issue, he lacks an agential history like mine, for example. And this is not a matter of his having an agential history of some other kind; he does not have an agential history of any kind at all. I offer a negative historical constraint on moral responsibility for actions and do not require that a being have a history as an agent before he can proceed to perform an action for which he is morally responsible because I leave it open both that instant agents are possible and that some of them are such that the first action they perform is one for which they are morally responsible.

Question 3. Why did you bother making the simple points you made so far in this section?

Your asking this question suggests that you would not raise the previous questions. Other people have raised them. I answer these questions as a means of preempting some misguided objections.

Question 4. Your main radical reversal stories feature extreme changes in a person's values. Why do you highlight such stories?

One function of these stories is to serve as counterexamples to various internalist claims, including claims by Harry Frankfurt quoted in Chapter 1. One wants one's counterexamples to be persuasive and intuitively powerful. The dramatic nature of the moral reversals in these stories helps in that regard.

Question 5. These same stories also feature people who successfully tried to make themselves as they were—before they were manipulated, that is. Why is that?

For the same reason. Take Sally. Even if she had just happened to be an extremely nice person (before being manipulated in the way she is in *One Bad Day* or *Bad Day Modified*) without ever having to work at it at all, many readers might confidently reject the claim that she is morally responsible for killing George. But the claim will seem even more preposterous to some readers when her story involves her having worked hard to make herself good. If it is replied that appearances here are misleading and that Sally is indeed morally responsible for killing George (in the original version of the story or in a version of the kind I just now mentioned), I am happy to entertain arguments for that position.

Question 6. In Chapter 2, you offered the following "radical reversal suggestion" about Sally in *Bad Day Modified*: "Sally's pre-transformation character was sufficiently good that killing George was not even an option for her; and the combination of this fact with the fact that Sally was morally responsible (to some significant extent) for that character, facts about her history that account for her moral responsibility for that character, facts about her post-manipulation character and associated abilities, and the facts that account for her killing George suffices for her not being morally responsible for killing him." Don't you commit yourself here to the positive historical claim that if Sally had not been morally responsible for her pre-manipulation character, she would have been morally responsible for the killing?

No. The quoted claim offers a *sufficient* condition for Sally's not being morally responsible for killing George. I do not claim that Sally's being morally responsible for her good character is a necessary condition for her not being morally responsible for killing George. Consider a story in which, as an unanticipated effect of an experimental drug that she was given at birth, Sally was blessed with a remarkable propensity for goodness, with the result that she effortlessly developed into an extremely good person. The remainder of this story—*Blessed Sally Gone Bad*—follows the lead of *Bad Day Modified.*[7] It may reasonably be claimed that Sally deserves no moral credit for her good character and that she is not at all morally responsible for that character in the present story. Even if this claim is correct, Sally is not morally responsible for killing George in *Blessed Sally Gone Bad,* as I see things; and, more important for present purposes, nothing I have said commits me to holding that she is morally responsible for killing him in this story. In *One Bad Day* and *Bad Day Modified,* the details that Sally was morally responsible for her character and that she worked hard to shape it are supposed to contribute to readers' confidence that she is not morally responsible for killing George in those stories. A factor that properly strengthens readers' confidence in this verdict does not have to be a necessary condition for the truth of the verdict. (A variety of facts justifiably contribute to my confidence that Michael Jordan was a great basketball player, including the following three: he was NBA finals MVP six times, he led the NBA in points scored for eleven seasons, and he scored over 30 points in 563 games. None of these accomplishments is a necessary condition for being a great basketball player.) And why do I care about readers' confidence in this verdict? Because I aim at persuading persuadable readers that the internalist thesis under consideration is false. Other things being equal, the more confident readers are that I am right about that, the better, as far as I am concerned.

Question 7. You just now said that in a variant of *One Bad Day* in which Sally's marvelous moral character was an accidental gift, Sally is not morally responsible for killing George. What recommends that judgment about *Blessed Sally Gone Bad*?

Here is a short answer that harks back to *DMR*. Sally's long-term pre-transformation character was sufficiently good that killing George was not even an option for her; by means of very recent manipulation to which she did not consent and for which she is not morally responsible, her system of values was suddenly transformed in such a way as to render killing George an extremely attractive prospect; the transformation ensures either (*a*) that although she is able during *t* intentionally to do otherwise than kill George during *t*, the only values that contribute to that ability are products of the very recent manipulation and are radically unlike any of her erased values (in content or in strength) or (*b*) that, owing to her new values, she has at least a Luther-style "inability" during *t* intentionally to do otherwise than kill George during *t*; and she killed George because of the manipulation. In my view, this collection of facts suffices for Sally's not being morally responsible for killing George.

Question 8. How do you respond to people who say that they don't share your intuitions about your good day and bad day stories and that they have the opposite intuitions from you about these stories?

Ideally, my response would be offered in a conversation. Early in that conversation, I would check to see whether my stories are being misunderstood. I would also try to get a sense of whether the interlocutor is bluffing. If the interlocutor has a good grasp of the stories and seems sincere, I would attempt to learn whether his or her verdicts about cases are shaped by unsubstantiated theoretical beliefs—for example, the belief that compatibilism commits its proponents to a brand of internalism that contradicts my verdicts about the stories or the belief that any acceptable theory of personal identity has the result that pre-manipulation Chuck and post-manipulation Chuck are two different persons. If the interlocutor persuades me that his or her verdicts about the stories are not products of suspect theoretical beliefs, are not symptoms of intuition deficit disorder (see Chapter 5), and express relatively pure intuitions, I would ask him or her to do something I have done. I have offered diagnoses of my having the intuitions I do about the stories at issue; these diagnoses provide statements of reasons supporting the verdicts I expressed about these stories. I would ask the interlocutor to do the same. With reasons for competing verdicts on the table, we can try to assess their relative merits. (For some discussion in this vein, see Chapter 3, Section 4.) Of course, the process might end in disagreement, but others who have witnessed the exchange of ideas may be in a position to carry the debate further. At the very least, they may express and explain their own judgments about the competing sets of reasons.

Question 9. Most of your stories about manipulation are not stories about the real world. That is, what happens in these stories never happens in the real world. So why should we care about these stories?

Robert Kane uses stories about manipulation in an argument for incompatibilism about free will (1996, pp. 64–72), and Derk Pereboom uses a well-known manipulation argument for incompatibilism about moral responsibility (2001, chap. 4, 2014, chap. 4). The main stories to which these arguments appeal are not real-world stories. If that is permissible, why? Because *conceptual* or *metaphysical* questions are at issue. What Kane and Pereboom are arguing, in effect, is that any proposed set of conceptually or metaphysically sufficient conditions for free will or for moral responsibility that is satisfiable in a possible world in which determinism is true falls short of sufficiency. If there really is no significant difference between the agents in their stories and any agent in a deterministic world, then if their agents are *possible* beings and lack free will and moral responsibility, they have made their point and it does not matter how far-fetched the cases are. We should care about such stories because of what they might tell us about free will and moral responsibility.

I myself have never considered replying to Kane and Pereboom that, because the arguments of theirs that I mentioned appeal to stories that are not real-world stories, those arguments should be ignored. Anyone inclined to respond in that way may find it interesting to try to construct a compelling argument for that response.

Question 10. Why haven't you discussed in this book the arguments you mentioned by Kane and Pereboom?

I have nothing important to add to what I said about them in Mele 2006 and 2007.

Question 11. Why don't you offer an analysis of an agent's being morally responsible for an action?

Given my agnostic stance on compatibilism about moral responsibility, if I were to undertake the task at issue, I would offer two analyses of an agent's being morally responsible for an action, one assuming the truth of compatibilism and the other assuming its falsity. So why don't I do that? If I were to offer an analysis—or two—of this, I would do so in the hope of persuading the great majority of readers that it—or one or the other of them—is true. What I am reporting is a fact about me. And I am not saying that I have the same hopes for all of my philosophical projects; I am talking specifically about analysis. Some philosophers might not have such high hopes for their attempted analyses, and some philosophers might have higher hopes than I would. Now, an analysis of moral responsibility for actions should accommodate widely shared, highly plausible intuitions about cases. And while I do hope that the great majority of my readers—on their own or with some help from me—accept the judgments I have made about cases in this book, I believe that there would be considerable disagreement about a range of other cases and that prospects for winning general acceptance of a view about assignments of moral responsibility in these cases are dim. As I see it, any attempt to push the analytical project to the boundaries of moral responsibility for actions will end in frustration.

Some philosophers have resisted an externalist view of the sort advocated in this book. And I have high hopes of persuading the great majority of readers that the externalist view advocated here is true. If I succeed at that, I will be extremely pleased. Obviously, success in this matter does not depend on my offering an analysis of moral responsibility for actions.

Question 12. Why don't you at least offer sufficient conditions for an agent's being morally responsible for an action? And why do you focus so tightly on a necessary condition for this—your negative historical condition?

My primary question in this little book, as I reported in the preface, is about vignettes featuring manipulated agents and vignettes featuring designed agents like Ernie. The question I posed there is this: What can we learn from vignettes of this kind about the nature of moral responsibility for actions? My answer, in a nutshell, is that we learn that moral responsibility for actions has a historical dimension. Reflection on agents with special properties motivated my negative formulation of the historical dimension. My primary opponents in this book are compatibilists who resist my externalism about moral responsibility for actions, though incompatibilists who resist it are also opponents. When opponents of either kind offer an analysis of moral responsibility that does not include a historical condition, we have something to argue about. But, depending on the details of the analysis, it may be that the *only* thing we have to argue about is whether a historical condition needs to be included. It may be that, from my perspective, the conditions some opponents offer in their attempted analyses are well on the way to being sufficient for moral responsibility for actions and all that needs to be added is a well-designed historical condition.

In short, I proceed as I do on the matters raised in the question at hand because I judged it best not to stray from the central task of this book. However, I should mention that I offer sufficient conditions for freely *A*-ing in Mele 2006 (pp. 200–201). In fact I offer four different sets of such conditions. They include two compatibilist sets—one for ideal agents and the other for ordinary agents—and two incompatibilist sets, one for each of the two kinds of agent, ideal and ordinary. All four sets share a negative historical element, and all four may be augmented to yield proposed sufficient conditions for moral responsibility simply by placing the actions at issue within the moral sphere.

5. DEALING WITH INCOMPATIBILISTS

An unusual feature of my position on moral responsibility and free will is agnosticism about compatibilism—in both connections, moral responsibility and free will (Mele 1995, 2006, 2017). While remaining neutral on whether compatibilism or incompatibilism is true, I have developed two sets of non-skeptical views of free will and moral responsibility—one for compatibilists (Mele 1995, 2006) and another for incompatibilists (Mele 1995, 2006, 2017). (These views have evolved over time.) As readers have noticed, I decided to focus the present little book primarily on the compatibilist side of things and on what we can learn about moral responsibility in particular (as opposed to free will) from reflection on stories about manipulation and related stories.

Obviously, I find the externalist compatibilist view developed here more attractive than competing compatibilist views. But I realize that not all compatibilists will share my attitude about this. This brief section addresses a question about fending off manipulation-based arguments against compatibilism (or against various compatibilist theses). Which sort of compatibilist view is better positioned to handle such objections—a conditional externalist view like mine or an opposing compatibilist view that embraces either unconditional internalism or a conditional externalism that does not extend to direct moral responsibility? For stylistic reasons, it is useful to have labels for the two types of view—mine and the alternative I mentioned. I unimaginatively dub the former *type 1* and the latter *type 2*.

An obvious point to make is that incompatibilists do not use particular stories about manipulation in arguments against compatibilism (or against various compatibilist theses) unless they find it intuitive that the agents in these stories are *not* morally responsible for the deeds at issue. My *type 1* view accommodates intuitions incompatibilists have about a range of manipulation stories and explains why compatibilists (*qua* compatibilists) are not committed to rejecting the pertinent nonresponsibility judgments. (This is not to say, of course, that my *type 1* view accommodates all incompatibilist intuitions about all manipulation stories.) Proponents of a *type 2* view obviously are in no position to take this tack in cases in which they reject the nonresponsibility judgments. If they want to persuade people who have the intuitions at issue—intuitions that I share—to endorse their *type 2* responsibility verdicts about cases, they have a burden I do not have.

At this point, it may be said that what matters is the strength of the arguments for various verdicts about cases. I have done what I can on that score. So, again, is a *type 1* or a *type 2* compatibilist view better positioned to fend off manipulation-based arguments offered by incompatibilists? Well, it is easier to accommodate the nonresponsibility intuitions that a *type 1* view accommodates and explain why compatibilism itself is compatible with the truth of the associated nonresponsibility judgments than it is to persuade incompatibilists that their intuitions about all the cases at issue are misleading or irrelevant. And there you have it.

What about compatibilists who say they find it intuitive that agents featured in such stories as the following are morally responsible for their featured deeds and who maintain that the corresponding responsibility judgments are true: *One Bad Day, Bad Day Modified, One Good Day, One Generous Day, One Good Deed,* and *Blessed Sally Gone Bad*? It may be said that they are in no position to accommodate the nonresponsibility intuitions at issue. If that is so, they have their work cut out for them. Should they become pessimistic about their prospects for success, they can take some comfort in my critiques of arguments to the effect that compatibilism itself—or any compatibilist position with a fighting chance—commits them to the pertinent responsibility judgments (see Chapter 4).

6. CONCLUSION

If the truth of compatibilism about moral responsibility for actions were to depend on the falsity of my conditional externalist view, then my verdicts about various stories—if those verdicts are correct—would falsify such compatibilism. *One Bad Day* and *One Good Day* are cases in point. However, as I explained in Chapter 4, extant arguments for a dependence thesis of this sort are unsuccessful, and I know of no superior arguments for theses of this kind. I explained as well that an externalist view of the sort advocated here is compatible with compatibilism. And I did not stop there. I offered grounds for believing that compatibilists about moral responsibility for actions should accept that view. So, I argued, should incompatibilist believers in such responsibility. What about agnostics about compatibilism who affirm the existence of moral responsibility for actions—people like me? Readers of this book know where I stand on the issue.

APPENDIX

Experimental Philosophy

Largely to check on whether my own intuitions about certain stories are out of line with judgments nonspecialists make about relevant cases, I conducted some simple studies. The results are reported and briefly discussed in this Appendix.

1. *Radical Reversals*

To gather evidence about how nonspecialists respond to radical reversal stories of the sort I have spun, I conducted a study that featured the following two stories.[1]

GOOD TO BAD

For a long time, Jones has enjoyed helping people. When he was much younger, Jones came to view himself, with some justification, as self-centered, petty, and somewhat cruel. However, Jones wanted to be the sort of person who does the right thing and helps others. He worked hard to improve his character, and he succeeded. Part of his strategy was to perform kind and generous actions with increased frequency in order to develop his sensitivity to others and his willingness to help. His strategy worked. He came to want to help people whenever he can, without any reluctance at all.

A team of scientists invented a machine that can duplicate one person's desires and values in another person. The scientists decide to use this machine to duplicate the desires and values of a very bad man, Smith, in Jones. When Jones went to bed last night, he was very kind and generous. But while Jones slept, the scientists duplicated

Smith's desires and values in Jones. They also erased all of Jones's desires and values that would have conflicted with those duplicated from Smith. The scientists made all of these changes to Jones's desires and values while leaving Jones's memory completely intact.

Jones wakes up with a desire to hurt people in his community by causing trouble for Girl Scouts and homeless people. Jones reflects on this desire and finds that this it fits very well with his system of values. He also concludes that he finally sees the light about morality: Morality is a system designed by and for weaklings. Upon reflection, Jones has no reservations about his desire to hurt people in his community; and given his values, Jones sees no good reason to refrain from hurting people. Jones devises a plan for what to do with his day: First, he finds a newly built Habitat for Humanity house in his neighborhood and vandalizes it. Then he drives around town for an hour and steals several boxes of Girl Scout cookies from helpless Girl Scouts—about fifty boxes in all. Finally, he steals all of the food and blankets from a local homeless shelter, and then destroys all of the food, blankets, and Girl Scout cookies in a giant bonfire. Jones identifies with his desire to hurt people and he hurts people because he wants to. When Jones falls asleep that night, the scientists undo everything they had done to him. When he wakes up the next day, he is just as kind and generous as ever.

BAD TO GOOD

For a long time, Smith has enjoyed hurting people. When he was much younger, Smith enjoyed bullying other children, but he was uneasy about that. His cruel actions sometimes caused him to feel guilty. He experienced bouts of squeamishness, and he occasionally considered abandoning his cruel ways. However, Smith valued being the sort of person who does as he pleases and who rejects conventional morality as a system designed for and by weaklings. He set out to ensure that he would be wholeheartedly behind his merciless bullying of vulnerable people. Part of his strategy was to perform cruel actions with increased frequency in order to harden himself against feelings of guilt and squeamishness and eventually to extinguish those feelings. His strategy worked. He came to lack any feelings of guilt or squeamishness about bullying people.

A team of scientists invented a machine that can duplicate one person's desires and values in another person. The scientists decide to use this machine to duplicate the desires and values of a very good man, Jones, in Smith. When Smith went to bed last night, he was very cruel and sadistic. But while Smith slept, the scientists duplicated Jones's desires and values in Smith. They also erased all of Smith's desires and values that would have conflicted with those duplicated from Jones. The scientists made all of these changes to Smith's desires and values while leaving Smith's memory completely intact.

Smith wakes up with a desire to help people in his community by doing volunteer work and making charitable donations. Smith reflects on this desire and finds that it fits very well with his system of values. He also concludes that he finally sees the light about morality, and he wants to be the sort of person who does the right thing and helps others. Upon reflection, Smith has no reservations about his desire to help people in his community; and given his values, Smith sees no good reason to refrain from helping people. Smith devises a plan for what to do with his day: in the morning, he starts working with a local Habitat for Humanity crew in his neighborhood. When the workday ends, he drives around town for an hour and buys several boxes of Girl Scout cookies from every Girl Scout he sees—about fifty boxes in all. Then he delivers the cookies to a local homeless shelter. Smith identifies with his desire to help people and he helps people because he wants to. When Smith falls asleep that night, the scientists undo everything they had done to him. When he awakes the next day, he is just as cruel and sadistic as ever.

Readers will have noticed that these two stories are toned-down versions of stories discussed earlier in this book. For example, there is no mention of killing in either new story. That is partly because I wanted the good and bad post-manipulation actions to concern similar subject matter in order to get a sense of whether people treat the two kinds of reversal—bad to good and good to bad—significantly differently. I also was independently disinclined to subject the participants to a story about killing.

Each participant read one story and was presented with four statements about it. Participants were asked to respond to each statement on a seven-point scale ranging from 1 (strongly disagree) to 7 (strongly agree). Two of the statements tested comprehension. One was about how the agent spent his day, and the other was about whether the agent worked on himself to become a person of a certain sort. Here are the other statements, two about Jones and two about Smith:

- J1. Jones is morally responsible for the bad things he does on the day described in the story above.
- J2. Jones deserves blame for the bad things he does on the day described in the story above.
- S1. Smith is morally responsible for the good things he does on the day described in the story above.
- S2. Smith deserves credit for the good things he does on the day described in the story above.

Responses from participants who failed one or both of the comprehension checks were excluded. Table A.1 presents the moral responsibility (*MR*) and desert (*D*) results for the remaining participants. Responses of 5, 6, and 7 are counted as representing agreement and responses of 1, 2, and 3 as representing disagreement. The majority of participants share my intuitions about these two stories. I do not

Table A.1 MORAL RESPONSIBILITY AND DESERT RESULTS

Moral responsibility

	Good to Bad	**Bad to Good**
MR: no	59.0%	56.9%
MR: yes	23.1%	26.4%
Group size	78	72

Desert

	Good to Bad	**Bad to Good**
D: no	64.1%	59.7%
D: yes	20.5%	23.6%
Group size	78	72

offer that fact in support of my externalist position; but if things had turned out otherwise, I would have been concerned.

2. *Non-moral Enhancement Stories*

In Chapter 3, in connection with Manuel Vargas's reported inclination to think that Chuck is praiseworthy for his good deeds in *One Good Day,* I suggested that it might be interesting to consider some roughly analogous cases from the non-moral realm. I commented briefly on the case of a novice at chess who plays very poorly. He receives a chip implant that gives him amazing chess skills for an hour, and in that hour he defeats a grand master in a brilliantly played game. I also commented on the case of an elderly man who blows away his powerful competition in a weightlifting match after aliens give him superhuman strength for a short time.

Discussion of my stories about chess and weightlifting with some philosopher friends motivated me to check my intuitions against those of nonspecialists. I used the following stories:

Chess Control. Jones is not very good at chess. But then a chess tutor teaches Jones how to play great chess. Jones plays a game of chess against a grand master. Each time Jones considers which move to make next, he focuses very hard on strategy and planning. Jones beats the grand master, and receives a trophy and a large cash prize for winning the game.

Chess Enhanced 1. Jones is not very good at chess. But some neuroscientists design a chip to make Jones into a chess expert for an hour, and they implant this chip into Jones's brain. Jones plays a game of chess against a grand master. Each time Jones considers which move to make next, he focuses very hard on strategy and planning. Jones beats the grand master, and receives a trophy and a large cash prize for winning the game. After the game, the chip stops working, permanently. Jones is back to normal.

Chess Enhanced 2. Jones is not very good at chess. But some neuroscientists design a chip to make Jones into a chess expert for an hour, and they implant this chip into Jones's brain. Jones plays a game of chess against a grand master. Each time Jones considers which move to make next, the chip tells Jones which move to make. Jones beats the grand master, and receives a trophy and a large cash prize for winning the game. After the game, the chip stops working, permanently. Jones is back to normal.

Weights Control. Many years ago, Jones was not very strong. But Jones then trained hard for years with the goal of becoming a champion weightlifter. After so many years of training, Jones enters a weightlifting contest and easily defeats everyone without trying hard at all. Jones receives a trophy and a large cash prize for winning the contest.

Weights Enhanced. Jones is not very strong. But some chemists design a drug to give Jones superhuman strength for an hour, and they inject it into his spine. Jones then enters a weightlifting contest and easily defeats everyone without trying hard at all. Jones receives a trophy and a large cash prize for winning the contest. After the contest, the drug stops working, permanently. Jones is back to normal.

Some of the participants saw just one case (either *Chess Control* or *Weights Control*), and the others saw two cases (*Weights Enhanced* and one or the other of the *Chess Enhanced* cases). All participants were asked to respond to a statement about desert and a statement about fairness on a seven-point scale. The statements were sometimes framed positively and sometimes negatively. They were as follows:

D1. Jones deserves the trophy and cash prize.
D2. Jones does not deserve the trophy and cash prize.
F1. It was fair for Jones to receive the trophy and cash prize.
F2. It was not fair for Jones to receive the trophy and cash prize.

In Table A.2, the desert and fairness responses are lumped together under the rubric "earned: yes/no." Here too, the majority of participants share my intuitions about these stories. As in the case of lay responses to the radical reversal stories, I do not offer this fact in support of my position, but if things had turned out otherwise, I would have been concerned.[2]

In Chapter 3, I reported my inclination to believe that readers who say that a novice deserves praise for defeating his opponent in stories like *Chess Enhanced 1* and 2 do not mean by "deserves praise" what I mean by it. The "earned: yes" responses to my enhancement stories about chess playing and weightlifting are in the ballpark of attributions of deserved praise. Perhaps the minority who give these responses—that is, who say that enhanced Jones deserves the trophy and cash prize or that it was fair for him to receive them—understand desert and fairness differently than I do. And perhaps discussion and reflection would move a substantial percentage of them over to my side. Something similar may be true of the minority who give the positive MR or D response to the radical reversal stories I tested. That is, they may understand moral responsibility and deserved moral blame and credit differently than I do, and perhaps discussion and reflection would modify their understanding of these things in my direction.

Table A.2 DESERT AND FAIRNESS RESPONSES

Chess

	Control	**Enhanced 1**	**Enhanced 2**
Earned: no	6.9%	75.0%	67.6%
Earned: yes	93.1%	15.9%	23.5%
Group size	29	44	34

Weights

	Control	**Enhanced**
Earned: no	13.0%	79.5%
Earned: yes	76.1%	12.8%
Group size	46	78

3. *More Figures*

Below are the mean (M) and standard error (SE) figures for the studies at issue in Tables A.1 and A.2.

Table A.1, moral reversal stories with separate MR and D results.
MR: Good to Bad. M = 3.179, SE = 0.219.
MR: Bad to Good. M = 3.319, SE = 0.233.
D: Good to Bad. M = 3.051, SE = 0.201.
D: Bad to Good. M = 3.222, 0.211.

Table A.2, non-moral stories.
Chess Control. M = 6.190, SE = 0.293.
Chess Enhanced 1. M = 2.455, SE = 0.238.
Chess Enhanced 2. M = 2.559, SE = 0.270.
Weights Control. M = 5.641, SE = 0.232.
Weights Enhanced. M = 2.359, SE = 0.178.

I mentioned (in note 2) that the enhancement stories were presented in two different orders. Some respondents saw one or the other of the enhanced chess stories first, and some saw the enhanced weights story first. Regarding responses to *Chess Enhanced 1* and 2: For participants who viewed one of these stories first, M = 2.634, SE = 0.258; and for participants who viewed one of these stories second, M = 2.351, SE = 0.271. Regarding responses to *Weights Enhanced*: For participants who viewed this story first, M = 2.054, SE = 0.256; and for participants who viewed it second, M = 2.634, SE = 0.243.

NOTES

Chapter 1

1. There are nonstandard definitions of "compatibilism" and "incompatibilism." I have never had a use for them.
2. The subjunctive conditional I quoted leaves it open that there are moral-responsibility-level free actions for which the agents are not morally responsible. Such an action may fail to satisfy a relevance requirement on moral responsibility to be described shortly.
3. In the philosophical literature on moral responsibility, blame normally is contrasted with praise. I have found that nonspecialists often view "praise" as too strong a term for the positive moral credit that people deserve for relatively modest good behavior. Given that my intended audience extends beyond specialists on moral responsibility, I have opted for contrasting blame with (positive) credit.
4. Even a little human being performing his first intentional action is influenced by things he has done. For one theory about important effects of movements we make before we are capable of acting intentionally on our subsequent intentional movements, see James 1907, chap. 26.
5. In Mele 2003a, I defend the thesis that to decide to *A* is to perform a momentary mental action of forming an intention to *A* (chap. 9) and I develop an actional view of deliberation (chap. 4).
6. How should such psychological truths as that at *t* Frank remembers that he saw a car accident yesterday be handled? If remembering that *p* entails *p*, then this truth is not silent on how Frank came to remember that he saw the accident.

It implies that a past car accident is among the causes of the memory at issue. However, the related psychological truth that Frank has at least an apparent memory of seeing a car accident yesterday is silent on how he came to be that way. It leaves various options open, including Frank's having hallucinated a car accident, an apparent memory of a car accident being implanted in Frank by a manipulator, and, of course, Frank's having seen a car accident yesterday.

7. A philosopher who endorses some conditional internalist thesis or other may also endorse unconditional internalism. Conditional and unconditional internalism are not mutually exclusive.
8. For data on lay judgments about cases of this kind, see Knobe 2003, pp. 317–18.
9. In responding to what Don Locke regards as an example of being morally responsible for an action one did not freely perform, Frankfurt writes, "Other things being equal, the [speeding] driver is no more blameworthy than if he had missed the child [who ran out from behind a parked car]; and he is far less blameworthy than someone who freely hits a child with his car. These considerations indicate that the speeder is not morally responsible for hitting the child at all. What he is responsible for is something like driving recklessly, and there is no reason to doubt that he does this freely" (1988, pp. 55–56). The same line may be taken on Van. It may be claimed that he is not morally responsible for killing the pedestrian and that he is morally responsible for something else—something that he does freely: perhaps driving drunk, or, if he is too drunk to be driving freely, getting drunk while believing that a consequence will be his driving drunk. In my view, a very common view, Van deserves to be blamed for the pedestrian's death, and that would not be so if he were not morally responsible for killing the pedestrian.
10. "Instant agents" is David Zimmerman's term for agents "who spring full-blown into existence . . . . Mele's 'Athena' and Davidson's 'swampman' are vivid examples" (1999, p. 252). For Athena and swampman, see Mele 1995, pp. 172–73 and Davidson 1987.
11. A specification of *W* may feature some part of *C*, following Frankfurt.
12. Section 2 of this chapter derives partly from Mele 2009a. For comments on a draft of that article or discussion of some of the ideas in it, I am grateful to Randy Clarke, Neil Levy, and Michael McKenna.

Chapter 2

1. In Mele 1995, I report that my belief requirement "on valuing is disjunctive: either *S* believes *X* to be good on balance or *S* believes *X* to be good without qualification" (p. 115).
2. In my view, intentional actions are caused; but, for certain dialectical purposes, I leave it open whether the causes include psychological states of agents (such

as values, in some cases), physical realizers of such states, or facts about what the agent desires, believes, intends, and the like. On this latitudinarianism, see Mele 2013a.

3. An incompatibilist about determinism and its having been open to a person to have desired something that he did not in fact desire claims that, in deterministic worlds, the only desires that it was open to an agent to have at a time are desires he actually had at that time. Compatibilists about the topic deny this. In this book, when compatibilism about moral responsibility is at issue, I assume that a compatibilist construal of the openness at issue is defensible—that is, that there is a defensible construal of the notion according to which an agent in a deterministic world could have desired something that he did not in fact desire.
4. Notice the active voice in my "people who suddenly and radically transform their values." Value transformations caused by brain tumors are another matter.
5. See Mele 2003b or 2017, chap. 4, for an examination of various ways of understanding what it is to be able to do something and various kinds or levels of ability.
6. Readers with concerns about the interpretation of "at *t*" in principles of this kind may wish to consult Mele 2006, pp. 15–16.
7. Readers who know that I have developed Frankfurt-style cases that I claim falsify *PAP* on various natural readings of it (Mele 2006, chap. 4; Mele and Robb 1998, 2003) may be puzzled by my openness to compatibilism about "could have done otherwise." (After all, Frankfurt-style cases are a driving force behind semicompatibilism.) To such readers, I point out that I nowhere claim that an agent's having been able to do otherwise than *A* is a necessary condition for his being morally responsible for *A*. Rejecting *PAP* is consistent with believing that there is an interesting sense of "could have done otherwise" in which agents in deterministic worlds sometimes could have done otherwise than they did. (For interesting traditional compatibilist reactions to Frankfurt-style cases, see Fara 2008, Smith 2003, and Vihvelin 2013.)
8. Frankfurt would not attempt to avoid this result by alleging insufficient psychic integration. Sally, in *One Bad Day*, is an agent of the sort Frankfurt has in mind in the following passage: "A manipulator may succeed, through his interventions, in providing a person not merely with particular feelings and thoughts but with a new character. That person is then morally responsible for the choices and the conduct to which having this character leads" (2002, p. 28).
9. I am grateful to Robert Wallace for suggesting a response to *One Bad Day* of the kind sketched here.
10. Some readers may think that what accounts for my intuitions that Sally and Ike are not morally responsible for their featured actions is the fact that *some other agent* is morally responsible for the pertinent features of these agents' internal conditions at the relevant time. They can easily be disabused of

this thought. Imagine that Ike's condition was produced by alcohol that magically appeared in his bloodstream out of the blue shortly before he started his car and that the sudden, radical change in Sally was caused by a brain tumor (see Mele 1995, pp. 168–69). Presumably, the great majority of readers who judge that these agents are not morally responsible for the featured actions in the original stories would make the same judgment in the modified stories.

11. For readers who wonder about values that are erased and then replaced with exactly similar values, I add that this trick is no part of Sally's story.
12. On these three kinds of analysis, see Sosa 2015, pp. 7–10.
13. For some evidence about folk attributions of moral responsibility, see Nahmias et al. 2005.
14. For a real-life case in which a brain tumor turned a man into a pedophile, see Burns and Swerdlow 2003. After the tumor was excised, the pedophilia (and related problems) disappeared. When the tumor returned, so did the pedophilia.
15. For a third point about Double's claim, see Chapter 4, Section1.
16. See, for example, Audi 1993, chap. 7; Ayer 1965, chap. 12; Grünbaum 1971; Mill 1979, chap. 26, especially pp. 464–67; and Schlick 1962, chap. 7. Also see Hume's remarks on the liberty of spontaneity versus the liberty of indifference (1739, bk. II, pt. III, sec. 2).
17. On coming to be a morally responsible agent, see Mele 1995, pp. 227–30, 2006, pp. 129–32, and 2017, pp. 211–17.
18. Even though the question is not rhetorical, the claim that every morally responsible human agent is such that the first thing for which he was (or is) morally responsible is a nonaction—for example, a nonactional omission or a desire—is hard to swallow.
19. If Davidson is right, swampman cannot perform intentional actions at the time he comes into being because, at that point, he lacks causal connections to the world needed for the possession of beliefs and desires (1987). When he first comes to exist, swampman has no thoughts at all, in Davidson's view (p. 444). In some designed instant agents, matters are different. See, for example, my discussion of minutelings in Chapter 3.
20. I briefly reply to worries about personal identity in Mele 1995, p. 175 n. 22. I return to this issue in Chapter 3.
21. By the way, have you, dear reader, ever had an urge to kill anyone? I never have (to the best of my recollection).
22. This chapter derives partly from Mele 2009a. For comments on a draft of that article or discussion of some of the ideas in it, I am grateful to Randy Clarke, Neil Levy, and Michael McKenna.

Chapter 3

1. See Mele 1995, p. 154, for a brief discussion of irresistible desires or Mele 1992, chap. 5, for a detailed discussion.
2. *NFM* is identical with a statement (*NF*) in Mele 2006 (p. 170), with one exception: *NFM* includes the words "and is not morally responsible for *A*-ing" (between "does not freely *A*" and condition 1).
3. Responsibility for this story is collective. Nathan Oakes suggested something like it that did not quite work. Carolina Sartorio improved it, as did Jason Turner, and I polished it a bit.
4. Someone might say "effortlessly"; but I regard that as a bit of an exaggeration, if the assertion is taken literally. If an agent expends some energy—no matter how slight—in pursuit of a goal, I count that as effort.
5. For any readers who believe that only decisions can be directly free, I add that I see no reason to believe that Sally's pertinent decisions—for example, a decision to give ten dollars to a homeless person she sees—are never directly free and never decisions for which she is directly morally responsible. And, of course, I have no inclination to believe that Chuck makes such decisions freely or is morally responsible for making them. Readers with the belief I mentioned about direct freedom should understand my use of "deeds" to include decisions.
6. Imagine a bad-to-good transformation story that features Chuck's being given a vivid vision of the Platonic Form of The Good for one day and his performing the good deeds described above. Would he be morally responsible for those deeds in this story? If someone were to explain the magic of The Good to me, I might be in a position to venture an answer. But notice that *One Good Day* is very different kind of story. Giving someone a vision of a Platonic Form is one thing; implanting values in him (after erasing his former values) is another.
7. Benjamin Matheson writes, "while Mele officially claims only to be offering a *negative* historical condition on moral responsibility, in the course of trying to persuade us that Chuck is, but Beth is not, morally responsible he illicitly appeals to a positive condition: that of having acquired one's unsheddable values under one's own steam," and he adds that "historicists are committed to the claim that a morally responsible agent—at least one who acts from unsheddable values—requires a past" (2014, p. 326). The errors here should be obvious by now. Beth's having acquired her unsheddable values under her own steam is part of what I claim to be a sufficient condition for her not being morally responsible for killing George. I nowhere claim that acquiring values—unsheddable or otherwise—under one's own steam is a necessary condition for being morally responsible for an action. Moreover, nothing that I have ever claimed commits me to holding that an instant agent—for example, a minuteling—who acts from unsheddable values is not morally responsible for the action.

8. "One kind of case I had in mind" is the expression I used to open the paragraph to which this note is appended. If Chuck's "rational control faculty" is to be counted as impaired, then *Thoroughly Bad Chuck* is a case of another kind I had in mind.
9. Obviously, being unable to do otherwise in my Luther-style sense does not require having made oneself this way.
10. I should note that the expression "*S* did not have time to shed *V* before he acted on it" is ambiguous. One reading takes the time *S* acted on *V* to be fixed. If *S* acted on *V* at noon, then, according to this reading, all that is being claimed is that *S* did not have time to shed *V* before noon. On another reading, the claim includes the idea that even if *S* had acted on *V* later than he actually did, he would not have had time to shed *V* before then.
11. There is a potential confound here. In the quoted claim at issue, Vargas offers a sufficient condition for a manipulated person's being "a morally responsible *agent*" (my emphasis). Someone who contends that Chuck is a morally responsible agent may consistently deny that he is morally responsible for his charitable deeds. Being a morally responsible agent does not entail being morally responsible for every intentional action one performs.
12. Responding to Mele 2009b, Vargas grants that "it is not obvious that we are anywhere near a stalemate" (2013, p. 296). Even so, the following points about the stalemate theme in Vargas 2006 merit attention.
13. Vargas reports that a revisionist theory will attempt to vindicate "historicist intuitions" if they are "justifiable and/or metaphysically innocuous" (2006, p. 361).
14. Enterprising readers may find clues about how to accommodate this judgment about Chuck in a Vargas-style view of moral responsibility in Vargas 2013, pp. 289–90.
15. Gary Watson writes, "The point of speaking of the 'real self' is not metaphysical, to penetrate to one's ontological center; what is in question is an individual's fundamental evaluative orientation. Because aretaic appraisals implicate one's practical identity, they have ethical depth in an obvious sense" (1996, p. 234). Practical identity should not be confused with personal identity, if Watson and I are right. The same goes for a person's moral character or moral personality.
16. Obviously, my claims here about the chess and weightlifting examples are about these particular cases of "enhancement." For an interesting discussion of another case of enhancement, see Vargas 2013, pp. 291–93.
17. For a penetrating critique of Sripada 2012 that applies directly to this contention, see Björnsson 2016.
18. This chapter is based partly on Mele 2009b and 2013d. I am grateful to Michael McKenna and Manuel Vargas for comments on a draft of the former article. Thanks are owed to Gunnar Björnsson for motivating me to write the

latter article, to Michael McKenna for comments on a draft of that article, and to Manuel Vargas for comments on Section 4 of this chapter.

Chapter 4

1. Ernie is intended to meet conditions I have proposed as sufficient (but not necessary) for being morally responsible for performing a given action if compatibilism is true (see Mele 2006, p. 188). Hence the reference to such things as ideal self-control and mental health in this story. Because, in Chapter 3, I announced my intention to leave my notion of unsheddable values behind, I deleted a sentence about such values.
2. More precisely, in my view, this is the line compatibilists who are not Humeans about laws of nature should take. On this, see Chapter 5, n. 7.
3. Soon, I will discuss a normally produced agent, Bernie, whose life mirrors Ernie's. Their internal conditions when they act mirror each other, as do their actions. Suppose that premise 2 is false and that although Bernie is morally responsible for some of his actions, Ernie is not morally responsible for anything he (Ernie) does. This supposed difference between the two agents would rest on a historical difference between them and therefore provide another route to an externalist view of moral responsibility. This is a route for philosophers who reject premise 2 to explore.
4. For related indeterministic cases of manipulation, see Mele 2006, pp. 139–44.
5. Watson's way of putting the "general point" is perhaps a potential source of confusion. Suppose that moral responsibility *does* have a necessary historical component. Call that component (or "constitutive condition") *H*. Provided that moral responsibility does not also depend on *another* historical matter, namely, the causes or causal origins of *H*, Watson's general point, as stated, may be true even given this supposition about *H*. That is, it may be true, even if externalism is true (in virtue of *H* being a necessary component of moral responsibility). However, I take Watson's "general point" to be intended as a statement of an internalist thesis. If I have caused any confusion just now, an analogy may prove useful. A necessary condition of something's being a sunburn is its being nondeviantly caused by exposure to the sun. This makes our concept of sunburn a historical concept. To find out whether sunburn is a historical concept, we do not need to look into *another* historical matter – namely, the causes or causal origins of something's being nondeviantly caused by exposure to the sun.
6. On capacities for control over one's mental life and bypassing, see Chapter 3, Section1. Recall the "full moon" story about Sally in Chapter 3, Section1, in which she is plausibly deemed indirectly morally responsible for killing George. In an analogous story, Chuck, from *Thoroughly Bad Chuck*, knows that there is a 10% chance that manipulators will turn him into a partial value

twin of sweet Sally for a day if he goes out under a full moon. Chuck despises the prospect of becoming a sweet person—even for a day—and he knows the moon is full tonight. But he sees a potential victim wandering in the street and, after reflecting on the cost to himself if he is manipulated, he ventures out to kill the man in the street, against his better judgment. As a consequence of Chuck's being out under a full moon, the manipulators work on him that night. The next morning, owing entirely to his new values, he does a good deed. In my view, Chuck has no moral responsibility for the good deed and deserves no moral credit for it. Thus, I am attracted to asymmetrical verdicts about moral responsibility in these two full moon stories.

7. If *NH* is not restricted to *directly* "free and responsible agency," it also is challenged—and, in my view, falsified—by pairs of stories like Van's and Ike's (two drunk drivers) in Chapter 1.
8. This is a theme in Russell 2010 as well.
9. This chapter derives from Mele 2016.

Chapter 5

1. As I observed in Mele 2006 (p. 190), although the argument for premise 2 sketched here sounds a bit like the consequence argument, it is significantly different. The consequence argument is an argument for incompatibilism. The argument for premise 2 is, by itself, consistent with compatibilism. The thesis that the cross-world difference in what caused *Z* does not support any cross-world difference in moral responsibility is consistent with Ernie's and Bernie's both being free and morally responsible agents, as is premise 2.
2. If Agnes were asked to identify a common feature of the two stories that supports her nonresponsibility judgments, she might say that, in both stories, Ernie is Diana's tool for getting things done that she wants to have done. In my deterministic story, she might say, Ernie is a perfect tool whereas in the indeterministic story he is a defective tool—a tool that might break down. She may view both kinds of toolhood as sufficient for Ernie's nonresponsibility for his actions.
3. The closest Fischer comes to a vignette like this in the article at issue is the following passage:

   And even if we changed the story to build into it that John and Mary had quite specific and even detailed desires with respect to the baby they hoped to create, this should not in any way affect our views about Ernie's moral responsibility 30 years later. It does not affect my evaluation of Ernie's moral responsibility, even if we add that John and Mary had sexual intercourse at the precise moment they did in the belief that, by so doing, they would ensure that Ernie would behave as he does in the future—perhaps even in the specific context in question some 30 years later. We could also

> add the supposition that, not only did they have intercourse with the relevant belief, but that John and Mary *intended* that their intercourse lead to Ernie's performing *A* and bringing about *E* 30 years hence. The intentions of John and Mary, and their acting in the belief that they are providing (relative to the background) a sufficient condition for something they want in the future, do not in any way bear on the intuitive basis for Ernie's moral responsibility in that context 30 years later. (2011, p. 268)

Consider just Ernie's doing *A* thirty years later. In my story, Diana exercises the power to intentionally bring it about that this happens and, indeed, the power to intentionally ensure that it happens. Her exhaustive knowledge of the state of her universe at a time and the laws of nature puts her in a position to do this. That is why the first step I took in augmenting Fischer's story was to bestow knowledge of this kind on John and Mary. Readers are invited to compare their intuitions about Ernie's *A*-ing in the story by Fischer quoted here with their intuitions about this in my augmented John and Mary story.

4. It is true that if a 75 pounder and a 71 pounder were each to lose 2 pounds, the former would still meet the weight requirement whereas the latter would not. But, of course, this difference between the two children does not warrant asymmetrical verdicts about whether the child who weighs 75 pounds and the child who weighs 71 pounds satisfy the weight requirement. (Jason Turner motivated me to add this note.)
5. Carolina Sartorio, a compatibilist, finds it intuitive that Ernie is not morally responsible and argues that the intuition is misleading (2016, pp. 159–70). For discussion, see Mele 2018.
6. I do not count Sally* (in whom a medium-strength urge to kill George is implanted in a story in Chapter 2, Section 4) as Sally.
7. As I pointed out in Mele 2006 (pp. 194–95), the truth of a Humean view of natural laws would undermine my thought experiment about Ernie. According to a Humean view, some of the ontological ingredients of the laws of nature of Ernie's universe—namely, future regularities—are not in place at the time of his creation. The natural laws might turn out to characterize a deterministic or an indeterministic universe, and even on the hypothesis that the universe turns out to be deterministic, it is open at the time of Ernie's creation precisely what its laws will be. So Diana, who is supposed to benefit from her knowledge of the laws of nature in designing Ernie, is in no position to know the laws of nature: Her complete knowledge of the past does not include knowledge of the laws; nor does it constitute a basis for deducing them. Even if Diana makes a true, educated guess about what the collection of natural laws will turn out to be on the basis of her complete knowledge of the past, it is open when she creates Ernie and right up to *t* both that she will be wrong about what the laws will be and that Ernie will not *A* at *t*. If Ernie were to *B* at *t*, something that is consistent with the entire past of his universe (given a Humean view of laws),

that fact would be one of the facts to be accounted for by a web of contingent generalizations that appear as theorems (or axioms) "in each of the true deductive systems that achieves a best combination of simplicity and strength" (Lewis 1973, p. 73): That is, it would be among the facts to be accounted for by the laws of nature. On a Humean view of laws, in Gideon Rosen's words, "it may turn out in the end [that] the laws are as they are in part *because*" Ernie acted as he did (2002, p. 705). Some agnostics about compatibilism may find themselves in that position partly because they are agnostic about Humeanism about laws of nature.

8. Readers should not confuse the theoretical boldness of a task with how time consuming it would be. Obviously, tracking down all the sets of jointly sufficient conditions for moral responsibility for an action ever proposed by compatibilists would be very time consuming.
9. I am not claiming that a soft-line reply to *ZAM* is not a viable option.
10. In Mele 2006 (p. 189), I wrote, "*the zygote argument* . . . runs, in skeleton form, as follows":
    1. Because of the way his zygote was produced in his deterministic universe, Ernie is not a free agent and is not morally responsible for anything.
    2. Concerning free action and moral responsibility of the beings into whom the zygotes develop, there is no significant difference between the way Ernie's zygote comes to exist and the way any normal human zygote comes to exist in a deterministic universe.
    3. So determinism precludes free action and moral responsibility.

    This conclusion is less modest than *ZAM*'s.
11. I presented a draft of an article (Mele 2013b) on which much of this chapter is based at a workshop on manipulation arguments at the Central European University (Budapest, Hungary). I am grateful to Ben Matheson and Kristin Mickelson for their commentaries, to the audience for their feedback, and to John Fischer, Ish Haji, Stephen Kearns, and Michael McKenna for discussion of some of the ideas in that article. Section 4 derives partly from Mele 2008, a draft of which was a topic of discussion on the "Garden of Forking Paths" blog. I am grateful to the discussants—especially, Neil Levy, Eddy Nahmias, Tim O'Connor, Derk Pereboom, and Paul Torek—for their comments.

Chapter 6

1. In later work, Kane distinguishes among "three freedoms" (2008, p. 142). He asserts that "Free acts may be"
    (1) acts done voluntarily, on purpose and for reasons that are not coerced, compelled or otherwise constrained or subject to control by other agents.

(2) acts [free in sense 1 that are also] done "of our own free will" in the sense of a will that we are ultimately responsible (UR) for forming.
(3) "self-forming" acts (SFAs) or "will-setting" acts by which we form the will from which we act in sense 2. (2008, p. 143, *sic*. On senses 2 and 3, also see Kane 1996, pp. 77–78.)

Kane observes that free actions of type 1, as he conceives of them, are compatible with determinism and that free actions of types 2 and 3 are not (2008, p. 143). All free actions of type 3, as Kane conceives of them, are indeterministically caused by their proximal causes, and only agents who perform free actions of type 3 can perform free actions of type 2.

2. Also see Kane 1999a, 2000, 2002, and 2011. Readers who balk at the thought that an agent may *try to choose to A* (Kane 1999b, pp. 231, 233–34, 2011, pp. 391–92, 2014, pp. 193–202, 208–209) may prefer to think in terms of an agent's trying to bring it about that he chooses to *A*.
3. Someone who contends that agents are morally responsible for all of their morally significant undetermined decisions will reject the claims I made in the paragraph to which this note is appended. But this contention is not credible. For example, relevant insanity would get an agent off the hook for some morally significant undetermined decisions. The same is true of some cases of manipulation.
4. There are also non-causal libertarians. For a critique of the thesis that uncaused actions done for reasons are possible, see Mele 2003a, chap. 2.
5. Some readers may see Chuck, in *Thoroughly Bad Chuck*, as only indirectly morally responsible for killing Don, on the grounds that showing mercy was not an option for him.
6. A referee asked for a fuller explanation. Here it is. *DMR* has the form "if *p*, then not *q*," where *p* is "an agent is directly morally responsible for *A*" and *q* is a long conjunction. Given Mabel's amazing powers, manipulators cannot bring about satisfaction of the fourth element of the conjunction. So "not *q*" will always be true of Mabel. Consequently, *DMR* is true of Mabel, because conditionals with true consequents are true.
7. Alexandra Pelaez and Mallory Madeiros are jointly responsible for my replacing, for aesthetic reasons, a benevolent alien with the drug.

Appendix

1. All studies discussed in this Appendix were conducted using Mechanical Turk.
2. In the study of enhancement stories, some participants responded to the enhanced weights story first and the others responded to either of the enhanced chess stories first. Here are the results by order of presentation.

	Weights 1st	**Chess 1st**	**Total**
Chess: not earned	70.3%	73.2%	71.8%
Chess: earned	13.5%	24.4%	19.2%
Group size	37	41	78

	Weights 1st	**Chess 1st**	**Total**
Weights: not earned	86.5%	73.2%	79.5%
Weights: earned	2.7%	22.0%	12.8%
Group size	37	41	78

REFERENCES

Audi, Robert. 1993. *Action, Intention, and Reason*. Ithaca, NY: Cornell University Press.

Ayer, Alfred. 1965. *Philosophical Essays*. London: Macmillan.

Barnes, Eric. 2015. "Freedom, Creativity, and Manipulation." *Noûs* 49: 560–88.

Björnsson, Gunnar. 2016. "Outsourcing the Deep Self: Deep Self Discordance Does Not Explain Away Intuitions in Manipulation Arguments." *Philosophical Psychology* 29: 637–53.

Burns, Jeffrey, and Russell Swerdlow. 2003. "Right Orbitofrontal Tumor with Pedophilia Symptom and Constructional Apraxia Sign." *Archives of Neurology* 60: 437–40.

Cappelen, Herman. 2012. *Philosophy Without Intuitions*. Oxford: Oxford University Press.

Davidson, Donald. 1987. "Knowing One's Own Mind." *Proceedings and Addresses of the American Philosophical Association* 60: 441–58.

Deery, Oisín, and Eddy Nahmias. 2017. "Defeating Manipulation Arguments: Interventionist Causation and Compatibilist Sourcehood." *Philosophical Studies* 174:1255–76.

Dennett, Daniel. 1984. *Elbow Room*. Cambridge, MA: MIT Press.

Double, Richard. 1991. *The Non-Reality of Free Will*. New York: Oxford University Press.

Dworkin, Gerald. 1988. *The Theory and Practice of Autonomy*. Cambridge: Cambridge University Press.

Fara, Michael. 2008. "Masked Abilities and Compatibilism." *Mind* 117: 843–65.

Fischer, John. 1994. *The Metaphysics of Free Will*. Cambridge, MA: Blackwell.

Fischer, John. 2000. "Problems With Actual-Sequence Incompatibilism." *Journal of Ethics* 4: 323–28.

Fischer, John. 2011. "The Zygote Argument Remixed." *Analysis* 71: 267–72.

Fischer, John, and Mark Ravizza. 1994. "Responsibility and History." *Midwest Studies in Philosophy* 19: 430–51.

Fischer, John, and Mark Ravizza. 1998. *Responsibility and Control: A Theory of Moral Responsibility*. New York: Cambridge University Press.

Frankfurt, Harry. 1969. "Alternate Possibilities and Moral Responsibility." *Journal of Philosophy* 66: 829–39.

Frankfurt, Harry. 1988. *The Importance of What We Care About*. Cambridge: Cambridge University Press.

Frankfurt, Harry. 2002. "Reply to John Martin Fischer." In S. Buss and L. Overton, eds. *Contours of Agency*. Cambridge, MA: MIT Press, 27–31.

Grünbaum, Adolph. 1971. "Free Will and the Laws of Human Behavior." *American Philosophical Quarterly* 8: 299–317.

Hume, David. 1739. *A Treatise of Human Nature*. Reprinted in Lewis Selby-Bigge, ed. *A Treatise of Human Nature*. Oxford: Clarendon.

James, William. 1907. *The Principles of Psychology*. New York: Macmillan.

Kane, Robert. 1985. *Free Will and Values*. Albany, NY: SUNY Press.

Kane, Robert. 1996. *The Significance of Free Will*. New York: Oxford University Press.

Kane, Robert. 1999a. "On Free Will, Responsibility and Indeterminism: Responses to Clarke, Haji, and Mele." *Philosophical Explorations* 2: 105–21.

Kane, Robert. 1999b. "Responsibility, Luck and Chance: Reflections on Free Will and Kane, Robert Indeterminism." *Journal of Philosophy* 96: 217–40.

Kane, Robert. 2000. "Responses to Bernard Berofsky, John Martin Fischer, and Galen Strawson." *Philosophy and Phenomenological Research* 60: 157–67.

Kane, Robert. 2002. "Some Neglected Pathways in the Free Will Labyrinth." In R. Kane, ed. *The Oxford Handbook of Free Will*. New York: Oxford University Press, 406–37.

Kane, Robert. 2008. "Three Freedoms, Free Will, and Self-Formation: A Reply to Levy and Other Critics." In N. Trakakis and D. Cohen, eds. *Essays on Free Will and Moral Responsibility*. Newcastle upon Tyne, UK: Cambridge Scholars Publishing, 142–62.

Kane, Robert. 2011. "Rethinking Free Will: New Perspectives on an Ancient Problem." In R. Kane, ed. *Oxford Handbook of Free Will*. New York: Oxford University Press, 381–404.

Kane, Robert. 2014. "New Arguments in Debates on Libertarian Free Will: Responses to Contributors." In D. Palmer, ed. *Libertarian Free Will*. Oxford: Oxford University Press, 179–214.

Kearns, Stephen. 2012. "Aborting the Zygote Argument." *Philosophical Studies* 160: 379–89.

Knobe, Joshua. 2003. "Intentional Action in Folk Psychology: An Experimental Investigation." *Philosophical Psychology* 16: 309–25.

Lewis, David. 1973. *Counterfactuals*. Cambridge, MA: Harvard University Press.

Matheson, Benjamin. 2014. "Compatibilism and Personal Identity." *Philosophical Studies* 170: 317–34.

McKenna, Michael. 2004. "Responsibility and Globally Manipulated Agents." *Philosophical Topics* 32: 169–92.

McKenna, Michael. 2008. "A Hard-Line Reply to Pereboom's Four-Case Manipulation Argument." *Philosophy and Phenomenological Research* 77: 142–59.

McKenna, Michael. 2009. "Compatibilism: State of the Art." *The Stanford Encyclopedia of Philosophy* (Winter 2009 Edition), Edward N. Zalta (ed.), URL = https://plato.stanford.edu/archives/win2009/entries/compatibilism/supplement.html

McKenna, Michael. 2012. "Moral Responsibility, Manipulation Arguments, and History: Assessing the Resilience of Nonhistorical Compatibilism." *Journal of Ethics* 16: 145–74.

McKenna, Michael. 2016. "A Modest Historical Theory of Moral Responsibility." *Journal of Ethics* 20: 83–105.

Mele, Alfred. 1992. *Springs of Action: Understanding Intentional Behavior*. New York: Oxford University Press.

Mele, Alfred. 1995. *Autonomous Agents: From Self-Control to Autonomy*. New York: Oxford University Press.

Mele, Alfred. 2003a. *Motivation and Agency*. New York: Oxford University Press.

Mele, Alfred. 2003b. "Agents' Abilities." *Noûs* 37: 447–70.

Mele, Alfred. 2006. *Free Will and Luck*. New York: Oxford University Press.

Mele, Alfred. 2007. "Free Will and Luck: Reply to Critics." *Philosophical Explorations* 10: 195–210.

Mele, Alfred. 2008. "Manipulation, Compatibilism, and Moral Responsibility." *Journal of Ethics* 12: 263–86.

Mele, Alfred. 2009a. "Moral Responsibility and Agents' Histories." *Philosophical Studies* 142: 161–81.

Mele, Alfred. 2009b. "Moral Responsibility and History Revisited." *Ethical Theory and Moral Practice* 12: 463–75.

Mele, Alfred. 2013a. "Actions, Explanations, and Causes." In G. D'Oro and C. Sandis, eds. *Reasons and Causes: Causalism and Anti-Causalism in the Philosophy of Action*. Basingstoke: Palgrave Macmillan, 160–74.

Mele, Alfred. 2013b. "Manipulation, Moral Responsibility, and Bullet Biting." *Journal of Ethics* 17: 167–84.

Mele, Alfred. 2013c. "Moral Responsibility and the Continuation Problem." *Philosophical Studies* 162: 237–55.

Mele, Alfred. 2013d. "Moral Responsibility, Manipulation, and Minutelings." *Journal of Ethics* 17: 153–66.

Mele, Alfred. 2015. "Free Will and Moral Responsibility: Does Either Require the Other?" *Philosophical Explorations* 18: 297–309.

Mele, Alfred. 2016. "Moral Responsibility: Radical Reversals and Original Designs." *Journal of Ethics* 20: 69–82.

Mele, Alfred. 2017. *Aspects of Agency*. New York: Oxford University Press.

Mele, Alfred. 2018. "Diana and Ernie Return: On Carolina Sartorio's *Causation and Free Will*." *Philosophical Studies* 175: 1525–33.

Mele, Alfred, and David Robb. 1998. "Rescuing Frankfurt-Style Cases." *Philosophical Review* 107: 97–112.

Mele, Alfred, and David Robb. 2003. "Bbs, Magnets, and Seesaws: The Metaphysics of Frankfurt-style Cases." In D. Widerker and M. McKenna, eds. *Moral Responsibility and Alternative Possibilities: Essays on the Importance of Alternative Possibilities*. Burlington, VT: Ashgate, 107–26.

Mill, John Stuart. 1979. *An Examination of Sir William Hamilton's Philosophy*. John Robson, ed. Toronto: Routledge and Kegan Paul.

Nahmias, Eddy, Stephen Morris, Thomas Nadelhoffer, and Jason Turner. 2005. "Surveying Freedom: Folk Intuitions About Free Will and Moral Responsibility." *Philosophical Psychology* 18: 561–84.

Pereboom, Derk. 2001. *Living Without Free Will*. Cambridge: Cambridge University Press.

Pereboom, Derk. 2014. *Free Will, Agency, and Meaning in Life*. Oxford: Oxford University Press.

Rosen, Gideon. 2002. "The Case for Incompatibilism." *Philosophy and Phenomenological Research* 64: 700–708.

Russell, Paul. 2010. "Selective Hard Compatibilism." In J. Campbell, M. O'Rourke, and H. Silverstein, eds. *Action, Ethics and Responsibility: Topics in Contemporary Philosophy*. Cambridge, MA: MIT Press, 149–76.

Sartorio, Carolina. 2016. *Causation and Free Will*. Oxford: Oxford University Press.

Schlick, Moritz. 1962. *Problems of Ethics*. David Rynin, trans. New York: Dover.

Schlosser, Markus. 2015. "Manipulation and the Zygote Argument: Another Reply." *Journal of Ethics* 19: 73–84.

Smith, Michael. 2003. "Rational Capacities, or: How to Distinguish Recklessness, Weakness, and Compulsion." In S. Stroud and C. Tappolet, eds. *Weakness of Will and Practical Irrationality*. Oxford: Clarendon, 17–38.

Sosa, Ernest. 2015. *Judgment and Agency*. Oxford: Oxford University Press.

Sripada, Chandra. 2012. "What Makes a Manipulated Agent Unfree?" *Philosophy and Phenomenological Research* 85: 563–93.

Strawson, Galen. 1986. *Freedom and Belief*. Oxford: Clarendon.

Strawson, Galen. 2002. "The Bounds of Freedom." In R. Kane, ed. *The Oxford Handbook of Free Will*. New York: Oxford University Press, 441–60.

Todd, Patrick. 2013. "Defending (a Modified Version of) the Zygote Argument." *Philosophical Studies* 164: 189–203.

van Inwagen, Peter. 1983. *An Essay on Free Will.* Oxford: Clarendon.

Vargas, Manuel. 2006. "On the Importance of History for Responsible Agency." *Philosophical Studies* 127: 351–82.

Vargas, Manuel. 2013. *Building Better Beings: A Theory of Moral Responsibility*, Oxford: Oxford University Press.

Vihvelin, Kadri. 2013. *Causes, Laws, and Free Will: Why Determinism Doesn't Matter*. New York: Oxford University Press.

Waller, Robyn. 2014. "The Threat of Effective Intentions to Moral Responsibility in the Zygote Argument." *Philosophia* 42: 209–22.

Watson, Gary. 1996. "Two Faces of Responsibility." *Philosophical Topics* 24: 227–48.

Watson, Gary. 1999. "Soft Libertarianism and Hard Compatibilism." *Journal of Ethics* 3: 353–68.

Zimmerman, David. 1999. "Born Yesterday: Personal Autonomy for Agents Without a Past." *Midwest Studies in Philosophy* 23: 236–66.

INDEX